"In this timely volume, Salberg and Grand expand the intellectual and moral frame of witnessing professionals to encompass transgenerational trauma in many cultures throughout the world. As they encourage us to face our own histories, including our own internalized perpetrators, they maintain our hope for a better world."

Judith L. Herman, M.D., author of *Trauma and Repair* and
Trauma and Recovery

"Salberg and Grand trace the psychical transformations of trauma theory from historical, antecedent and embryonic versions to mature conceptual renditions of ideas in this relatively new domain of psychoanalytic inquiry. The result is a rich account that lends itself to the teaching of psychoanalytic concepts and to clinical practices where narratives of generational trauma show themselves. The authors' consistently lucid clinical narratives, in particular, display phenomena that are engaging, powerful, and, above all, demonstrate why this new domain deserves every attention it now commands."

Maurice Apprey, Ph.D., D.M., F.I.P.A., Professor Emeritus
of Psychiatry, University of Virginia School of Medicine,
and Training and Supervising Psychoanalyst, Contemporary
Freudian Society

"In their important new book, Jill Salberg and Sue Grand deepen our understanding of the transgenerational legacies of trauma by taking us beyond the binary of victim and perpetrator. Full of rich and evocative examples, Salberg and Grand demonstrate what it means to recognize and disclose the traumas that reside within us. They address descendants of victims and perpetrators alike, and show us how to hold the complexity of these positions, rather than side with one over the other. Our conversation will become much richer as a result. *Transgenerational Trauma: A Contemporary Introduction* is a significant contribution and essential reading for anyone who is interested in understanding how today's crisis-ridden world has been shaped by legacies of trauma."

Roger Frie, Professor of Education,
Simon Fraser University

In their book, *Transgenerational Trauma: A Contemporary Introduction*, Jill Salberg and Sue Grand move beyond the classical silence of the analyst, towards the empathic dialogic internal listening and witnessing that is essential to relieve psychic pain. Grounded in relational and attachment theory, they offer a historical and theoretical journey through our field's transgenerational resistances to exploring trauma as a dynamic and analytic entity. Salberg and Grand share their and other clinicians' narratives with poignancy and nuance, capturing the affective resonance and necessary engagement that transforms both members of the analytic couple. Created as a teaching series, it does that and much more.

Dionne R. Powell, author of *From the Sunken Place to the Shitty Place: The Film GetOut, Psychic Emancipation and Modern Race Relations from a Psychodynamic Clinical Perspective* (Psychoanal. Q.), Co-Chair of the Holmes Commission on Racial Equality in American Psychoanalysis

"No topic is more urgent and timely in contemporary psychoanalysis than the transgenerational transmission of trauma. In this volume, two leading lights, Jill Salberg and Sue Grand, provide a scholarly yet readable overview of the breadth and depth of the field. The theoretical chapters are interspersed with moving personal testimonials. While attentive to the legacies of perpetrators as well as victims, the authors never lose sight of the beacon of social justice that guides them in their clinical odysseys."

Peter L. Rudnytsky, Head, Department of Academic and Professional Affairs, American Psychoanalytic Association, and author of *Mutual Analysis: Ferenczi, Severn, and the Origins of Trauma Theory*

Transgenerational Trauma

In this book, Jill Salberg and Sue Grand offer an overview of the psychoanalytic work on transgenerational trauma, rooting their perspective in attachment theory, and the social-ethical turn of Relational psychoanalysis.

Transgenerational Trauma: A Contemporary Introduction is a cutting-edge study of trauma transmission across generations. Salberg and Grand consider how our forebears' trauma can leave a scar on our lives, our bodies, and on our world. They posit that, too often, we re-cycle the social violence that we were subjected to. Their unique approach embraces diverse psychoanalytic and psychodynamic theories, as they look at attachment, legacies of violence, and the role of witnessing in healing. Clinical and personal stories are interwoven with theory to elucidate the socio-historical positions that we inherit and live out. Social justice concerns are addressed throughout, in a mission to heal both individual and collective wounds.

Transgenerational Trauma: A Contemporary Introduction offers a nuanced and comprehensive approach to this vital topic, and will be of interest to psychoanalysts, psychologists and other mental health professionals, as well as students and scholars of trauma studies, race and gender studies, sociology, conflict resolution, and others.

Jill Salberg is Faculty at the New York University Postdoctoral Program in Psychoanalysis. She is the editor of *Psychoanalytic Credos: Professional Journeys of Psychoanalysts* (2022) and *Good Enough Endings* (2010).

Sue Grand is Faculty at the New York University Postdoctoral Program in Psychoanalysis. She is the author of *The Hero in the Mirror: From Fear to Fortitude* (2009) and *The Reproduction of Evil* (2002). She has co-edited two books with Lewis Aron and Joyce A. Slochower: *Decentering Relational Theory: A Comparative Critique* and *De-Idealizing Relational Theory: A Critique From Within* (both 2018).

Jointly they are the editors of *Wounds of History: Repair and Resilience in the Trans-Generational Transmission of Trauma* (2017) and *Transgenerational Trauma and the Other: Dialogues across History and Difference* (2017), both won the Gradiva award in 2018.

Routledge Introductions to Contemporary Psychoanalysis

Aner Govrin, Ph.D.
Series Editor

Tair Caspi, Ph.D.
Executive Editor

Yael Peri Herzovich, Ph.D.
Assistant Editor

"Routledge Introductions to Contemporary Psychoanalysis" is one of the prominent psychoanalytic publishing ventures of our day. It will comprise dozens of books that will serve as concise introductions dedicated to influential concepts, theories, leading figures, and techniques in psychoanalysis covering every important aspect of psychoanalysis.

The length of each book is fixed at 40,000 words.

The series' books are designed to be easily accessible to provide informative answers in various areas of psychoanalytic thought. Each book will provide updated ideas on topics relevant to contemporary psychoanalysis – from the unconscious and dreams, projective identification and eating disorders, through neuropsychoanalysis, colonialism, and spiritual-sensitive psychoanalysis. Books will also be dedicated to prominent figures in the field, such as Melanie Klein, Jaque Lacan, Sandor Ferenczi, Otto Kernberg, and Michael Eigen.

Not serving solely as an introduction for beginners, the purpose of the series is to offer compendiums of information on particular topics within different psychoanalytic schools. We ask authors to review a topic but also address the readers with their own personal views and contribution to the specific chosen field. Books will make intricate ideas comprehensible without compromising their complexity.

We aim to make contemporary psychoanalysis more accessible to both clinicians and the general educated public.

Aner Govrin – Editor

Transgenerational Trauma: A Contemporary Introduction
Jill Salberg and Sue Grand

Transgenerational Trauma

A Contemporary Introduction

Jill Salberg and Sue Grand

R Routledge
Taylor & Francis Group

LONDON AND NEW YORK

Designed cover image: Michal Heiman, Asylum 1855–2020, The Sleeper (video, psychoanalytic sofa and Plate 34), exhibition view, Herzliya Museum of Contemporary Art, 2017

First published 2024
by Routledge
4 Park Square, Milton Park, Abingdon, Oxon OX14 4RN

and by Routledge
605 Third Avenue, New York, NY 10158

Routledge is an imprint of the Taylor & Francis Group, an informa business

British Library Cataloguing-in-Publication Data
A catalogue record for this book is available from the British Library

ISBN: 978-0-367-54140-8 (hbk)
ISBN: 978-0-367-54142-2 (pbk)
ISBN: 978-1-003-08776-2 (ebk)

DOI: 10.4324/9781003087762

Typeset in Times New Roman
by codeMantra

Contents

Introduction[1]

Recently, there has been interest in the transgenerational transmission of trauma, clinically and culturally. How do the ghosts of our forebears flow through us? How are we compelled by their un-mourned pasts? Does knowing this history facilitate healing? This literature opens up these questions. We have often collaborated in this area—in a conference on the "wounds of history"; in our papers and in our books (e.g., Grand & Salberg, 2015; Salberg & Grand, 2017)—as well as individually in our own papers and books. Our work has been particularly inspired by Maurice Apprey, Judie Alpert, Haydee Faimberg, Roger Frie, Sam Gerson, Adrienne Harris, Judith Herman, Lynne Layton, Dori Laub, Kirkland Vaughans, and other colleagues too numerous to name here. We are indebted to those who have entrusted us with their stories and to those who held our stories in their minds.

All of this work is informed by an ethic of social justice. In addressing social violence, this literature draws on a long tradition in psychoanalysis, which began with our psychoanalytic forebears and partakes of the recent social-ethical turn in Relational psychoanalysis. The result is an evolving theoretical expansion of psychoanalysis, shaped by family, culture, history, and politics. It is our belief that psychoanalysis has long been too narrowly defined by the white, Viennese, male Jewish mind of Freud and his followers, as well as by a code of loyalty in succeeding generations. The Interpersonal and Relational theoretical perspectives critiqued many of these traditional tenets, broadening the field to include the subjectivity of the analyst and the effects of cultural, Feminist and racial critiques, along with querying gender theory and the whiteness of psychoanalysis. The renewed emphasis on trauma has brought dissociation and enactment into the foreground.

DOI: 10.4324/9781003087762-1

This book introduces the reader to this expansive field of trauma and its transgenerational transmission. We begin with the history of this field, highlighting its roots in diverse theoretical traditions. We situate transgenerational transmissions within the history of attachment theory and research; we explore the categories of victims and perpetrators and illuminate the role of witnessing in healing. We have found that this expanding field forces psychoanalytic theory to change, to be cracked open.

To that end, later chapters elucidate the theoretical biases of psychoanalysis and ask how these limitations are still embedded in the transgenerational literature. What happens when these universalist assumptions encounter non-Western, non-white patients and cultures? Whose histories are present in this literature, and whose histories are still absent? We hope that our readers will join us in this critical engagement. To answer social violence, a great multiplicity of voices is necessary, and psychoanalysis needs to query itself.

To move toward social justice, we need to know our own histories and the histories of others. In particular, we need dialogues across difference. The co-authors come to this topic with our own *similar* transgenerational histories. We have carried the weight of our forebears; we have been inspired by them, and we are aware that our own cultural context can limit our vision. We are both white, Jewish, American urban women, descendants of Eastern European Jews fleeing from anti-Semitism. We were both born in the 1950s. We were trained at a progressive, psychoanalytic institute in NYC. Despite our lifelong social justice orientation, we have been embedded in a white, middle-class psychoanalysis. We can only speak and read English, a peculiarly American tendency. Embarking on this project, we realized we would only be able to review literature in English. Whose work would be presented in this review, and whose would be excluded because it is not translated into English? Whose voices would be silenced? Would we reproduce some of the harm done that we address in this volume? With our linguistic and cultural limitations, this seemed inevitable. This recycling of harm done is part of transgenerational transmission, as we discuss later in this text. In joining with you, the reader, we can keep creating antidotes to this social violence. We can fortify the resiliency we inherited from our forebears and maintain hope for a just world.

Note

1   We are indebted to Kristopher Spring for his editorial expertise throughout this book.

Legacies of Trauma Histories

Melancholic Hunger

Michael O'Loughlin[*]*: Personal Story*

I grew up in Ireland with parents three generations removed from The Great Famine of 1845–1852. The Famine was devastating to the poorer classes, leaving more than one million dead from starvation and related diseases, and another three million fleeing, many of them in the steerage compartments of coffin ships. Further losses were produced by the severance of social linkages and genealogical filiations due to the erasure of the Irish language.

I was born into a family descended from the poorest classes of Irish people. With parents who lacked formal education or social capital, the best we could do was keep body and soul together and strive for any economic foothold we might be able to gain. Born into *bare life*—life as biological necessity rather than as a place of existential possibility— abetted by an Irish Catholic fatalism and a decided lack of focus on interiority or emotional validation in school, like so many others I was bereft. My father, born in 1921, grew up on a subsistence farm, consisting of 20 acres of barren bogland. He tried to scrape together a living there for himself and his new wife, my mother. My father could only purchase his weekly pack of cigarettes from a traveling vendor if he had sufficient eggs to barter. All of his siblings had migrated to London, and he remained at home as the designated caretaker to his aging parents. His father was an alcoholic, and by all accounts, his mother suffered severe paranoid psychosis. At least two of my father's siblings suffered from alcoholism and both died in poor circumstances in London. My father suffered significant anxiety throughout his life, including severe panic attacks. My mother, too, grew up destitute. She lost her mother early and the family was so poor that she and her sister attended school on alternate days because they had only one

DOI: 10.4324/9781003087762-2

presentable frock to wear between them. "There wouldn't be any point in me talking to you," she said when I sought to interview her, "because I couldn't tell you the bad things. They are too awful. I wouldn't want anyone to know them." She was not persuaded by my argument that it would be helpful to me in understanding myself and understanding how I came to be. She spoke repeatedly of the daily humiliations of rural poverty, repeatedly prefacing her remarks with "You won't believe this" or "I can't believe we had it that hard."

David Lloyd captures this melancholic residue of silence and shame:

> The silence is at once the silence of depopulation and the silence of a traumatized culture; the wail is the almost animal wail of despair and passivity before a catastrophe that seems to exceed comprehension. Wordless, the wail is also anonymous, without any distinct human voice to utter it. As a recurrent motif of the Famine it marks simultaneously the dissolution of the Irish as makers of their own culture and history and the historical emergence of a new kind of Irish identity whose elements are in many respects still present and which embodies a peculiar weave of memory, damage and modernity.
>
> (1997 p. 33)

Troubled with such knowledge, I have struggled to reclaim voice, not only for myself, but for my parents and forebears, and by definition, for all who experience, marginality, displacement, and erasure in our unequal world.

Note

* Michael O'Loughlin is Faculty in Psychology and Education and in the Postgraduate Programs in Psychoanalysis and Psychotherapy at Adelphi University, New York.

1

Historical Overview of Theories of Trauma and Transgenerational Transmissions

Jill Salberg

Early Theories of Trauma: Freud's and Ferenczi's Perspectives (Europe 1880s–1939)

Over the past three decades, there has been a steady increase in the growing body of literature in psychoanalysis on the transgenerational transmission of trauma. This expanding field grows out of interdisciplinary work drawn from trauma studies, psychoanalysis, neuroscience, epigenetics, as well as critical race and gender theories. In this opening chapter, I will be tracing the history of how trauma appears, disappears, and reappears in the theoretical architecture of the field. Until trauma became fully understood as a critical subject of psychoanalysis, a theory of multiple generations and the transmission of traumatic experiences, affects, and disturbances could not be fully formulated.

Psychoanalysis has repeatedly been divided in its attempts at conceptualizing the genesis of human suffering. From the outset, a prevailing idea in early theories was that feelings or experiences that were unbearable for a person to know resulted in there being a "splitting of consciousness." While there is a strong trend within the field to locate the earliest ideas on trauma with Freud (1856–1939), it is perhaps more accurate to start with Pierre Janet (1859–1947), a contemporary of Freud. Janet's early work focused on dissociative states of mind in patients suffering from hysteria, which he termed "*dédoublement de la personnalité*" (Janet, 1886) and simultaneously the existence of "*idée fixes*," which Howell and Itzkowitz (2016) write, "refer to dissociative phenomena, such as thoughts, mental images, intense emotions, and related behavioral actions, that play a major role in hysterical crises, i.e., traumatic re-enactments (Janet, 1889, 1898)" (p. 22). These early ideas of Janet suggest a very prescient sense of the effects of trauma

DOI: 10.4324/9781003087762-3

on the mind, and yet Janet's work did not become the early basis of the growing field of psychoanalysis.

The earliest of Freud's writings (1894) only briefly mention Janet and Binet as influences on his and Breuer's understanding of hysteria and the splitting of consciousness. The many patients that Freud and Breuer would write about in their *Studies in Hysteria* (1895) point to traumatic experiences resulting from what Freud would refer to as his "seduction hypothesis" (what today we would call rape or childhood sexual abuse). However, this was short-lived as a theory that saw the effects of trauma happening in the external world affecting the minds of mostly children and young women. Both Freud and Breuer turn away from further investigating their insight that trauma is causative of emotional/mental distress. However, they disagreed over Freud's growing insistence on the role of sexuality, and by the time *Studies in Hysteria* was published they were no longer working together or even speaking. This split was further completed when Freud wrote to Fleiss, who came to replace Breuer as Freud's confidante, that he no longer believed in his "seduction hypothesis." He concluded that this must be the fantasy life of the child that the adult is recalling during their treatment.

One might say that splitting has been operative in psychoanalysis from its inception, particularly its long and complicated relationship with trauma and its complexity. Freud's turning away from his seduction hypothesis has been argued at length as to his motivations, both personal and professional. Most relevant here is that it created a split between a psychoanalysis based fundamentally on internal processes—a world populated by phantasies, drive derivatives, defense mechanisms, and conflicting forces—and a conception of trauma as a real-world event inevitably affecting a person and their mind. Freud thus developed his major conceptualizations of the internal world of the mind, something that had not been done by any of the other early physicians of that day. While a theory of the unconscious had already been part of the scientific discourse at that time (see Ellenberger, 1970), Freud created an entire theory of mind unlike anything else that came before. He focused on the unconscious and its effect on consciousness and behavior. This early model of mind, Freud's topographical model, described the ways in which consciousness and unconsciousness were separated by defensive forces of repression and yet were in a dialogic tension.

However, despite the enormity of his genius and creation, trauma—as an external event, be it sexual assault, or of historical/political, economic, or social forces—never became part of what he considered to be psychoanalytic. This becomes most evident in the rift that formed with one of his colleagues (also briefly a former patient) and another beloved confidante, Sándor Ferenczi. While Freud's zeal was toward development of a scientific theory of mind, Ferenczi was dedicated to healing the wounds of his patients. This is most evident in their letters during World War I and their postwar papers.

Freud spent the war years in Vienna, worried about his sons who were in the military and writing his major papers on metapsychology. These papers remain some of his most important works, establishing his evolving model of mind, which would completely become revamped as his structural model of mind (id, ego, and superego). Freud insisted on a distinction between what he termed *actual neurosis* and the neurosis of defense, the *psychoneuroses* that consumed Freud's thinking and writing. He conceived of these as completely different categories, placing neurasthenia and hypochondria in the former and hysteria and obsessional neuroses in the latter. Freud was theory-building; his emphasis was on the sexual instinct and defenses against it. It is noteworthy that although Freud was also writing about treatment and technique, he was less disrupted in his thinking if a patient did not improve, believing it was a result of resistance or what he would later term *negative therapeutic reaction*.

Today, we might consider the role of trauma, its disabling impact on the survivor, and the complex process needed to heal and recover. Ferenczi spent the war early on stationed at battlefields and then in a hospital treating soldiers wounded and suffering from what was then termed *shell shock*. His early paper, "Two Types of War Neuroses" (1916/1917), is a very moving account of his work with patients suffering from the horrors of World War I. His careful and detailed descriptions of the tremors, tics, paralyses, phobias, and other symptoms are some of the earliest documentations of shell shock. Today, these symptoms would be diagnosed as PTSD, while Ferenczi termed it traumatic *anxiety hysteria*. Clearly, trauma was seen as causative, and Ferenczi's tone in his writings is one of deep care and horror over the awful and cruel damage wrought by the war on the soldiers. These experiences would carry over to and inform Ferenczi's sense of the injured traumatized child within the adult patient.

It is also worth noting that Freud was of a generation of Jews afforded entry into educational/university settings and middle-class professions for the first time. In today's world, we'd view this as entry into white Western privilege and, with that, an adoption of the biases and prejudices that the majority society had toward *others*. The *other* is always in reference to whiteness but also to maleness; colonization is thus seen within the psychic realm as a further frontier of patriarchy. This resulted in women, people of lower class or impoverished people, and people of color and/or darker skinned peoples from what today would be called the 'developing world' were cast in Freud's theories as non-normative, that is, non-white male.

Celia Brickman's (2018) work details Freud's absorption of colonialist and racist points of view, seeing indigenous peoples as "primitive" and uncivilized, which he then likens to the forces in the unconscious. In failing to take the sociopolitical and historical into account, Freud's theories embedded racist, sexist, and classist biases into his theories. Brickman writes: "Freud worked within a conceptual network strongly influenced by the late nineteenth-century racist anthropology which had helped legitimate Europe's colonizing and slaving enterprises" (p. xviii). Brickman doesn't want Freud's work to be discarded, but read, contextualized, and understood as representing normality as equated with dominant cultural. Further, Gaztambide (2019), while agreeing with Brickman's reading, believes it was even more complex for Freud. Drawing upon historical studies of colonization and early proto-capitalistic enterprises, Gaztambide argues,

> Skin color informed class, and later textured race. We find then, an organizing principle of power and control that lasted centuries and generations—the "other," whether coded in terms of race or class (and we can add gender and sexuality as well), is "black," wild, dangerous, irrational, primitive, and in need of external control and domination. By contrast, the "self" is pure, white, rational, controlling, dominant, and civilized.
>
> (p. 8)

Black psychoanalysts have long understood the whiteness and bias in psychoanalytic theories. Jones (2015) argued that: "It is time for the field to pursue one of Freud's deepest wishes, and that was for his creation to be more than a practice restricted by ethnic and racial concerns (pp.723).

Freud can be regarded as the marginalized Jew, embedded in anti-Semitic cultural tropes (Gilman, 1993), such as racialization of the Jew as dark or black (associated with Africa) and as degenerate (sexually) and inferior/emasculated males. These stereotypes imprisoned Jews for many years in ghettos and denied them entry into educational and professional opportunities (Salberg, 2007). Emancipation helped to lift these strictures while anti-Semitism waned, but the hatred resurged in the form of genocidal violence (pogroms and the Holocaust). It is also important to note that Freud and many of the early analysts did ascribe to political and social justice values. It is easy to perhaps overlook that this was once fully part of psychoanalysis, given the emphasis on intrapsychic processes that took precedence within the field post-World War II.

Freud's trauma theories changed from a seduction theory (trauma experienced from an external source) to the trauma being internally caused by fantasies and an ego insufficiently developed to regulate libidinal or aggressive fantasies. It is with Ferenczi that we can see more of an acuity toward the patient's sufferings or neuroses resulting from real-life traumas, be it violence as in war (1916/1917), abusive neglect by parents (1929), or sexual abuse by family or significant others in the child's life (1933/1949). Mészáros (2018) has written that "Ferenczi developed new perspectives on trauma that were radical and profound enough to be deservedly called a *paradigm shift* in trauma theory" (p. 115). Further, Rudnytsky (2022) would argue that Ferenczi and his patient Elizabeth Severn (known in his Clinical Diary as R.N. and while in her treatment with him their brief experimentation with "mutual analysis") wrote in their individual psychoanalytic papers "a fully elaborated *trauma* and not a "seduction" theory…they went far beyond Freud (pp. 1–11)." Ferenczi, in believing that his patients had been sexually abused by an important grown-up in their life and simultaneously denied acknowledgment of the trauma by others, created a new space to think about how external events impact us and how they become internalized and part of the internal world. I want to underscore the enormity of this divergence from Freud and the alteration of psychoanalytic understanding.

> Through the identification, or let us say, introjection of the aggressor, he disappears as part of the external reality, and becomes intra- instead of extra-psychic; the intra-psychic is then subjected, in a dream-like state as is the traumatic trance, to the primary process, i.e., according to the pleasure principle it can be modified or changed by the use of positive or negative hallucinations. In any case the attack as a rigid external reality ceases to exist and in the traumatic trance the child succeeds in maintaining the previous situation of tenderness.
>
> (Ferenczi, 1933/1949, p. 228)

Ferenczi's focus on real acts carried out by grown-ups put him in opposition to Freud's insistence on unconscious fantasy, as did his resolve about the harm caused by adults' disavowal and denial. Ferenczi's prescient understanding of the traumatizing impact of the refusal of acknowledgment by those whose care matters the most to the child is what I would see as a *failure of witnessing*, a profound underemphasized part of trauma. Freud's reaction to Ferenczi's ideas—and the forces that Ernest Jones would later bring to bear, including only publishing his work in German and not in English in the *IJP* and spreading rumors that Ferenczi had a mental collapse—allowed the suppression of Ferenczi's work for many decades after his death. This permitted psychoanalysis to develop without a fuller recognition of the significance and reality of trauma, while trauma studies and the intergenerational transmission of trauma would later develop and evolve as an area of study outside the field of psychoanalysis.

With Ferenczi's work there is a new, transformed conception of mind and the world. It is now conceived of as an active interchange between a child's experience of real-life trauma and betrayal and the mental attempts to process this without benefit from significant adults. We are told that external events can impact internal processes, and a new mechanism, identification with the aggressor, causes introjection. The suppression of perhaps Ferenczi's most important and valued work kept it outside of psychoanalytic scholarship for years to come, a further splitting within the field of psychoanalysis and perhaps a place marker of trauma within the field. Balint (1968/1979) has written "The historic event of the disagreement between Freud and Ferenczi acted as a trauma on the psychoanalytic world" (p. 152). He further describes how constricted the field became around alterations in technique and understanding of the usefulness of regression in psychoanalysis.

Ferenczi's Legacies and Influences in the U.K. and the U.S.

Ferenczi's work was suppressed by Ernest Jones and not published for a long time; his reputation was maligned (see Rachman, 1997). Nonetheless, looking back, we can see his influence and the seeds of his ideas. Michael Balint was one of his most famous students, analysand, close friend, and literary executor. Balint left Budapest in 1939, settling in the UK, first in Manchester and then later moving down to London. It is as a result of his consistent and indefatigable efforts to bring Ferenczi's ideas, papers, and influence back into psychoanalysis, efforts to repair the trauma of him being attacked and cast out, that we owe an enormous debt. Balint held back translation and publication of Ferenczi's "Confusion of Tongues" paper into English until 1949, when he believed it would be better received; it appeared in the *International Journal of Psychoanalysis*. Balint's own work (1968/1979) furthered Ferenczi's early ideas on regression and trauma. Throughout his papers and chapters, you see him fervently citing and arguing the merits of Ferenczi's discoveries and the limits in classical Freudian thinking and technique. Balint joined the Middle Group, now known as the Independent Group, at the British Society after the Controversial Discussions.[1] He aligned with Fairbairn, Winnicott, and Bowlby; these were all analysts who moved away from drive theory, focusing on early mother–child relationships, trauma, and the fuller theorizing of object relations theory (see Ricaud, 2018).

Ferenczi's influences are seen in the work of Melanie Klein in ways that extend and differ from him, her first analyst. His writings on projection and introjection were precursors to Klein's fuller elaboration of the internal world of the infant. Minuchin (2018) believes his influence was equally formative on Klein's emotional growth as she struggled with a deep depression following her mother's death and her difficult marriage. Perhaps equally important, though, were Ferenczi's ideas concerning early maternal deprivation and/or trauma. Kohon (1986) has written,

> Ferenczi's concept of "early maternal deprivation," and his notion that object relations exist even in the deepest layers of the mind, were the theoretical background that allowed the ideas of Melanie Klein, Michael Balint, Ronald Fairbairn and Donald Winnicott and others to develop.
>
> (p. 21)

This focus can be seen as well in Bowlby's development of attachment theory and the concept of a safe base, the infant/child's need to find/ return to the mother or primary caregiver during times of fear. The resulting experience of feeling "safe" and comforted then allows the infant to resume exploring the world. Equally important to note is that Klein remains within a one-person conceptualization of mind, consistent with Freud's drive theory, and one of the fiercest proponents of the death instinct. The others, Balint, Fairbairn, Bowlby, and Winnicott, each had some aspect of a two-person psychology in their work.

Winnicott's ideas certainly elaborated further on the interchange between the world and the child. This can be seen most directly in his conceptualization of fear of breakdown and catastrophe. Winnicott understands that impingement—seen as experiences of unthinkable or archaic anxiety, of excess before there is a self that can think or manage it, before the baby/child has a sense of going-on-being—will cause a splitting of the self and the creation of a false self in the aftermath of trauma. Maternal deprivation is a focal point in Winnicott (1967):

> The feeling of the mother's existence lasts x minutes. If the mother is away more than x minutes, then the imago fades, and along with this the baby's capacity to use the symbol of the union ceases. The baby is distressed, but this distress is soon *mended* because the mother returns in $x + y$ minutes ... the baby has not become altered. But in $x + y + z$ minutes the baby has become *traumatized* ... the mother's return does not mend the baby's altered state. Trauma implies that the baby has experienced a break in life's continuity, so that primitive defenses now become organized to defend against a repetition of "unthinkable anxiety" or a return of the acute confusional state that belongs to disintegration of nascent ego structure.
>
> (p. 369)

The influence of Ferenczi can be seen in France and the United States, where psychoanalysis took root and/or was brought by émigré analysts escaping Nazi Germany, deadly anti-Semitism, and the war. I will discuss the seeds of Ferenczian ideas in France in the next section, when I explore the earliest writing on intergenerational transmissions. As for the United States, Ferenczi's influences can be appreciated through his analysand Clara Thompson and later Erich Fromm. Harry Stack Sullivan had heard Ferenczi give a talk in 1926 at the New School in New York. He was very interested in Ferenczi's ideas on severe trauma, and while he couldn't afford to go to Europe to be analyzed, he urged his close colleague Clara Thompson to do it in his stead and bring Ferenczi's ideas and techniques back. Sullivan's plan was for Thompson to then analyze him and help heal his serious early trauma. Thompson did go, first for two summers, 1928 and 1929. She found these sessions very useful, and in 1931 she moved to Budapest for more treatment and training. She remained there in treatment with Ferenczi until his death.

In writing about her analyst's contribution to psychoanalysis, Thompson acknowledges the extent that Freud overshadowed and derided some of Ferenczi's unique work, referring to his ideas on technique and theory as "not psychoanalytic," a phrase that continues today in the field as a harsh regulatory authoritarian measure.[2] The most important themes from her analysis with Ferenczi that Thompson drew upon seem to come from his relaxation therapy. She, along with Sullivan, Fromm, and others, broke away from New York Psychoanalytic Institute and the orthodoxy of that institute to form the New York branch of the Washington Institute, later renamed the William Alanson White Institute. Thompson has written about the real personality of the analyst, of sincerity and the analyst's ability to be honest when making mistakes and genuine in giving love and affection to the patient. All of these ideas can be seen in the work of Ferenczi (1932/1995) in his *Clinical Diary*.

With the translation and release of Ferenczi's *Clinical Diary*, the rediscovery of his work on trauma and alteration of technique became more widely available and known. This catalyzed a kind of paradigm shift away from classical Oedipal interpretation-focus to earlier pre-Oedipal material; from internal conflict to acceptance of the effects of external trauma on mind and greater acceptance of what had been a more interpersonal and interactive treatment approach. This further resulted in shifting psychoanalysis expansively toward an intersubjective model of mind and technique. Thompson was clearly influenced in this direction, bringing to Interpersonal psychoanalysis an emphasis on two people in the interaction (patient and analyst) and the real relationship that develops along with the transferential one. However, Shapiro (1993) believes that Thompson failed to fully bring Ferenczi's emphasis on trauma and the denial by the parents, which was traumatizing to the child, into her work and writings.

Erich Fromm was also influenced by Ferenczi's work and championed him. He cited Ferenczi and challenged the negative campaign that Ernest Jones had led against Ferenczi's reputation. Fromm was influenced by the Frankfurt School's beliefs that individuals were formed by social structures and not the reverse. He was critical of Freud's theories, likening them to attitudes and morals found in bourgeois/capitalistic society. Additionally, Fromm stressed Ferenczi's urging of love and empathy toward patients and that analysts should admit their mistakes to their patients. Bacciaguluppi (1993), in writing about Ferenczi's influence on Fromm, translated a quote from a German language paper that Fromm wrote right after Ferenczi died:

> Ferenczi's premature death is a tragic end to his life. Torn between his fear of a rupture with Freud and the realization that a departure from Freud's technique was necessary, he did not have the inner

strength to pursue the road to the end. His contrast with Freud is a contrast in principle: that between a human and friendly approach, which affirms unconditionally the analysand's happiness, and a patricentric-authoritarian "tolerance," which deep down is hostile.

(pp. 187–188)

Further, Bacciagaluppi argues that Ferenczi's influence spread to the British Middle School and to the American Interpersonal School but with different emphases; as a result, there were few contacts between these two locales and no cross-fertilization.

Transgenerational Transmission Theories

In many ways, psychoanalysis during the 20th century became shaped by social and political trauma, by the historical forces of the political revolution in Russia, the rise of communism, fascism, World War I and II, and a genocidal form of anti-Semitism that culminated in the Holocaust. The mass emigration that ensued, as these waves of upheaval and destruction spread, disrupted the nascent and growing psychoanalytic movement originally centered in Vienna, with centers also in Berlin and Budapest. There were two main waves that saw émigré analysts leave the main psychoanalytic centers. The first wave was after World War I (1918–1921), and the second was in the years preceding World War II and following the end of the war with the survivors of the Holocaust (which included those from concentration camps, those who went into hiding, and those who actively worked in the resistance). Émigré analysts who escaped had to contend with immigration quotas in both London and the United States, while others found their way to South America.

A large percentage of these émigré analysts were Jewish, fleeing the Nazis and certain death. Kuriloff (2013) has studied the silence of the émigrés, who did not discuss their experience of the Holocaust and trauma they endured, nor did they ask about it in sessions with patients who fled and survived. She noted that our analytic theories show a lack of evidence—or perhaps it is more appropriate to say a *missing presence*—of what had just transpired and been endured. Survival of these traumas left an imprint in both what couldn't be spoken about for a long time as well as the resilience that many found to withstand atrocity and creative attempts to maintain their humanity. Ornstein (2004) wrote that she drew upon her fantasy life to withstand the brutality of life in Auschwitz. However, the catastrophe of Europe during those years and the destructive violence directed at Jews was appallingly absent in the writings and work of a group who were overwhelmingly Jewish. Prince (2009) has argued that psychoanalysis itself was traumatized by the Holocaust:

> Psychoanalysis is a survivor of the Holocaust. It was founded and flourished in central European centers that would be destroyed by the Nazis. A core group of refugees who lived through persecution and exile were instrumental in rebuilding their movement on alien shores.
>
> (p. 179)

Aron and Starr (2013) extended Prince's (2009) idea of psychoanalysis itself as a trauma survivor, arguing that it was born out of trauma to begin with and grown during the developing seeds of virulent anti-Semitism in a Europe pervaded by enduring racism, misogyny, and homophobia. While we now can consider this silence a response to trauma, a dissociative gap that enabled people to try to recreate their lives, the psychoanalytic canon at that time did not include these kinds of ideas.

It is interesting to posit that, with any trauma, it often takes the passage of time before processing can take place. Time was certainly needed for metabolizing the trauma of the Holocaust in order to be able to study it, and perhaps this further delayed a more generalized transgenerational transmission study of other historical traumas. Davoine (2007) believes that it takes half a century to process a war, suggesting an even longer gestational period of silence. It is therefore noteworthy when theories of transmission from one generation to the next occurs. It is in the early papers by Nicolas Abraham and Mária Török in French and their collected writings *The Shell and the Kernel* (1994) that we can begin to see the influence of Ferenczi and the Hungarian school.

Both Abraham and Török were Hungarian-born Jews: He emigrated to Paris in 1938 before the war, and she came to Paris after the war in 1947. They both trained in France and met each other at the Sorbonne in the early 1950s. Their book is a collection of their individual and joint papers that explore aspects of Freud and Ferenczi's theories, also drawing upon Klein. While neither of them personally knew Ferenczi, Rand (1994) believes that their endeavor, like Ferenczi's, was to draw upon Freud's earliest ideas of childhood seduction and how causative trauma is in the development of neuroses. Their goal is that a person's life story should lead the analysis and not theories. It is in this way they critique Freudian theory and simultaneously expand it.

Their most original idea, *transgenerational haunting*, which they refer to as the *phantom*, was developed to understand symptoms such as phobias and obsessional behaviors. They wrote about phantoms as magical solutions to mourning that had been denied and refused. Drawing upon Ferenczi's conceptualization of introjection, Török sees the theoretical thread from Ferenczi's (1926) original conceptualization of introjection as a way that the outside world gets taken inside the ego. Freud (1917) had expanded on Ferenczi's idea in "Mourning and Melancholia," theorizing how loss of the object can be denied by incorporating the object within the ego through the process of identification. Török argued that some losses can be seen as trauma denied, and it is incorporation of the object, distinguishing it from introjection, which allows a fantasy to become installed, entombed as it were, in the unconscious. Rand (1994) introduces this idea as

the obstacles to introjection include the phantom, an undisclosed family secret handed down to an unwitting descendent; the illness of mourning, which [Abraham & Török] define as bereavement complicated by an untoward sexual outburst in the mourner at the time of loss; incorporation, or the secret and vital embrace of an alien identity; and the secret, or crypt, which "entombs" an unspeakable but consummated desire.

(p. 16)

These "entombed" secrets disrupt development and become ghostly presences transmitted to the next generation. They never directly wrote about the war in Europe nor about their experience of being Jews during the virulence of anti-Semitism that resulted in Hitler and the Nazi's genocidal attempt to kill off the Jews in Europe. They also didn't speak of their having to leave their homes in Hungary and emigrate, yet these social and political forces can be seen in their emphasis on external traumas and losses that cannot be known and truly mourned. Their reconceptualization of psychoanalytic theory, as Ferenczi's before them, does not rely on drives or primary narcissism but on real events within a family and the world.

Around the same time frame in the United States, Selma Fraiberg, Edna Adelson, and Vivian Shapiro (1975) had started an Infant Mental Health Program. In their now classic paper, working within a traditional Freudian model, ghosts of the parents' unremembered past were placing their children in dire jeopardy, necessitating non-traditional home treatment interventions in families.

> Our hypothesis is that access to childhood pain becomes a powerful deterrent against repetition in parenting, while repression and isolation of painful affect provide the psychological requirements for identification with the betrayers and aggressors ... In each case, when our therapy has brought the parent to remember and re-experience his childhood anxiety and suffering, the ghosts depart, and the afflicted parents become the protectors of their children against the repetition of their own conflicted past.
>
> (pp. 420–421)

I believe that this work rested upon the assumption of the crucial nature of secure, safe attachment. Given the traumatic physical and sexual abuse in the history of the parents they worked with, they were intervening to prevent transgenerational transmissions of not only fear and anxiety, but of actualizing violent behavior. Their ideas and interventions were remarkably prescient of where the field would later be moving toward.

The next entry point of transgenerational transmission theories is the painful process of Holocaust survivors' symptoms, testimony, and witnessing projects in the United States. Analysts did not start writing about the effects of World War II and Holocaust-related trauma on psychoanalytic theory and practice for quite some time—until, as Laub and Auerhahn (1993) suggest, subsequent analytic generations started to metabolize this wound of history. Bergmann and Jucovy (1982) have some of the earliest writings in psychoanalysis regarding the effects of the Holocaust on its survivors in the early 1960s and on the second generation several years later. Bergmann and Jucovy (1982), Grubich-Simitis (1984), Kestenberg (1982), Krystal (1985), and others were being quite revolutionary in their writing that trauma, writ large in reality, could impact the mind of someone and affect their relationships. While Abraham and Török were also writing about this, their work was not translated yet into English. It is undoubtedly an understatement to say that both World War I and II massively disrupted tens of thousands of lives, and we can see how theories are starting to process these traumas and account for disruption now being seen in what came to be known as "the second generation."

In 1967, the International Psychoanalytical Association held the first symposium on this topic, "Psychic Traumatization through Social

Catastrophe." Early contributors found common features in survivor families. Kestenberg (1982) investigated the effects of the Holocaust on the second generation, highlighting the idea that survivor-parents can transmit conflict and psychopathology to their offspring as a result of their own trauma incurred during the Holocaust. Kestenberg, along with Epstein (1979), initiated scholarship on the transgenerational transmission of Holocaust-related traumas to subsequent generations.

Despite their utilizing classical theoretical interpretative concepts, Big History was beginning to be formulated as an important context within which to understand psychic life. The wealth of data furnished by Laub's (1989, 1992, 1995) work taking video testimonies (which began in 1979), including his co-founding the Fortunoff Video Archive of Holocaust Testimonies at Yale University, also greatly advanced what we could learn about the impact of Holocaust trauma on survivors and their families. Laub (2017) was not only a dedicated psychiatrist/psychoanalyst, but also, as is well-known, a child survivor and a child of a Holocaust survivor.[3] Laub (1989), director and primary investigator for the video testimony project at Yale University's Genocide Studies Program, coined the poignant phrase *the empty circle*, drawing on a dream element of one of his patients. The motif of *the empty circle* captured "the absence of representation, the rupture of the self, the erasure of memory, and the accompanying sense of void that are the core legacy of massive psychic trauma" (p. 507). Despite knowledge of their parents' trauma, Laub found that the children of trauma survivors experience a hole, an absence, in their family members' survivor stories and minds.

Additionally, I want to underscore that traumatic states are not the only transmissions that are occurring. They are noteworthy because of their disruptive effect and the ways in which they rupture attachment. But to leave the impression, as a great deal of the Holocaust literature does, that trauma and damage pervades all of the survivor's life and their children's mind has rightly been criticized (see Ornstein, 2003; Richman, 2006). Richman (2006), in reviewing Anna Ornstein's (2004) poignant memoir, urges us to see that the thinking in the field has suffered by its being dichotomous regarding trauma, that is identifying who was damaged from who was resilient. I have come to believe that this is once again a form of splitting endemic to our minds and our theories. A move towards inclusiveness requires an end to splitting, and as Grand (2018b) wrote:

> We cannot fail to honor real human resilience, as it exists, during and after trauma, in the living and in the dead. But all too often we

have an either/or vision of the human spirit. Either is dead or alive. Either it is evacuated or it is heroic ... In my view, neither alone is an adequate rendering of traumatic experience ... [nor] honors the nuances of survival. Both polarities can represent a failure of recognition, de-individuating those who have already been objectified.

(p. 11)

With all of the work done on the Holocaust, it is noteworthy that it didn't create an equal opening and study on the near genocide of the native peoples in the lands where colonization occurred (as in the United States, Caribbean islands, Mexico, South America, and Australia, to name a few), the enslavement of Africans and their ongoing exploitation of chattel slavery and its legacy of racism, anti-Asian laws, and the violence and persecution of non-white peoples in general. Every episode of mass violence is enabled by willful obliviousness and collective denial. In its aftermath, there is often a shared incapacity to bear, understand, or begin to process the enormity of atrocity. Silence often continues to be the response by the world. Survivors of the Holocaust were oppressed by this silence; people of color continue to be. Many survivors of genocide or mass trauma are flooded by memories and compelled to speak to their children; others never utter a word. In the aftermath of atrocity, survivors' children must navigate their particular parental predicament. They often must do so in cultures that do not offer a reflective, recognizing container for this Big History.

The Holocaust focused psychoanalysts on the capacity for genocidal hatred and on the effects of this violence on survivors. This focus has now, within the past two decades, expanded our look at other ongoing examples of human cruelty: political purges and violent wars, slavery and its legacy in racism, sexual abuse of children and sexual trafficking, hatred of sexual differences and gender differences, as well as all persecutory forms of xenophobia. We (Grand & Salberg, 2015; Salberg & Grand, 2017) have focused our work on these issues, investigating the legacy of this mass violence across generations. We are deeply engaged by and concerned about what will be transmitted to later generations: both our patterns of destructiveness *and* our patterns of resiliency.

While good work has been done in the fields of trauma, witnessing, and psychoanalytic theory, this work needs to be updated by the newer models of mind that are shifting our more traditional paradigm. How will remembrances be symptomatized, repeated, and transformed? I have come to think about psychic pain and symptoms, interpersonal difficulties, the psyche/soma connection, social links, and Big History as intersecting threads. These threads shape, and are shaped by, culture, race, and gender in an interpenetrating loop.

While the study of the transgenerational transmission of trauma began with a look at Holocaust trauma, rich work in this field continues (Gerson, 2009; Grand, 2009; Grand & Salberg, 2015; Guralnik, 2014; Harris, Kalb, & Klebanoff, 2016; Richman, 2006). It has been in the past 20 years that scholarship on witnessing, testimony, and transgenerational transmission has extended beyond the Holocaust to other political and social traumas and genocides. Thus, we have work by Apprey (2003, 2017), Gump (2010), and Leary (2002, 2012) on the legacy of African American slavery in subsequent generations; Davoine and Gaudillière (2004) linked the inchoate memory of World War II with psychosis in subsequent generations; Faimberg's (1998, 2005) idea of "telescoping of generations"; and Reis' (2005) efforts to expand analytic conceptions of the patient's history past consideration of a person's developmental course to include the shaping force of events in creating culture or the very subjects that experience culture and cultural events. Another way trauma entered psychoanalysis was through the very important work with the survivors of childhood sexual abuse (see Alpert, 2017; Davies & Frawley, 1994; and others). This work emphasized dissociation and the internalized object relations between victim, bystander, and perpetrator. Returning to the early work of Freud and to the clinical perspective of Ferenczi, this literature ignited an expansive look at dissociative processes. Grand (2000) has examined the legacy of the Armenian genocide, as well as the transgenerational transmission of genocide through the perpetration of sexual abuse on succeeding generations; she (2015) has also examined the racial legacy of Native American "vanishing" in the United States and linked this to African-American slavery. Vaughans (2015) has written about the long-term effects of slavery, expanding the "cultural introject" concept affecting the lives of blacks and whites today. I (Salberg, 2015) have written about how the attachment relationship is the mode of transgenerational transmissions and carries the presence and absence of parental dysregulation resulting from traumatic experiences.

Faimberg's (1996, 1998, 2005) extensive work investigates these intergenerational occurrences, seeing them as narcissistic identifications of the child's mind by the parents' unsettling affects. She explores the effects that the Holocaust and emigration have had on multiple generations and how the historical context of such a large trauma makes demands on our minds. Faimberg found in her patient Mario someone absent from his own life and experience—while he was in fact present in the secret lives of his parents prior to his own birth, her concept of the "telescoping of generations." For Faimberg (2005), the interior of the child of a trauma survivor is not so much empty as it is filled with a condensed history of the parent, causing an "alienated identification" in the child: "The identifications constitute a 'link between generations,' which are alienating and opposed to any psychic representation" (p. 15). She sees understanding the internal response not so much as a pathologizing of the survivor but as a complex inner world of attempts to know and un-know affects and experiences simultaneously. I would consider this as efforts toward transforming the trauma.

Furthermore, Faimberg believes that the child inhabits an unacceptable part of the parent, an unconscious *not-me* experience. This is quite close to what Bromberg (2006, 2011) explicates in his work on dissociative experience, attachment, and relational trauma. Both Faimberg and Bromberg utilize and extend Sullivan's (1953) early concept of *not-me* personifications to highlight and explain dissociative transmissions. Undergirding this is Sullivan's early focus on transmissions of anxiety through the mother–child bond starting in infancy, believing it to be a key disruptive factor. Harris (2007) invokes Abraham and Török (1994) in discussing Davoine's (2007) therapeutic work that tracks history, war, and multiple internal worlds:

> Once you begin to think this way about the shadowy line between the living and the dead, about the active absence and presence of spectral figures in our consulting rooms, in our dream lives, and in our lives, a rich experience of self and others opens up.
>
> (p. 663)

I (Salberg, 2015) believe that this occurs to an even greater degree if trauma underpins the anxiety and becomes part of the fabric of the mother-child attachment. Further expansion of our psychoanalytic model from the family of origin into what Salberg and Grand (2017) referred to as *a transgenerational turn* into a transgenerational model. Acknowledging the impact of multiple generations and siblings would make psychoanalysis less hierarchical and expand its theorizing horizontally.

Further, psychoanalysts such as Apprey (1999, 2003, 2014) see links between the traumatic effects of the Holocaust and the trauma of slavery, writing about transgenerational hauntings and errands that one generation installs in the unconscious of the next (see also Grand, 2000, 2014; Grand & Salberg, 2015; Gump, 2000, 2010, 2017; Harris, Kalb, & Klebanoff, 2016; Salberg, 2015; Salberg & Grand, 2017). Relational trauma theory is rooted in the social world, in the collective experience of persecution and trauma as in ethnic genocide, sexual abuse, and political and racial abuses. This literature embraces the psychic, the interpersonal, and the collective; it attends to both the micro and maxi levels; and it entwines several critical threads. These threads include the nature of dissociation; the internalization and repetition of victim-bystander-perpetrator dynamisms; the nature of "sanity" and "madness"; attachment and intersubjectivity; somatic and procedural communication; and the function of witnessing. These themes have drawn on existent theory, but they have also reshaped our theory as we think about trauma transmissions (see Davoine & Gaudillière, 2004; Grand, 2000, 2009, 2018b; Guralnik, 2014, 2016; Layton, 2006, 2020; Reis, 2005; Thomas, 2009). Davoine and Gaudillière have been at the forefront of examining this kind of social link, seeing how history has been a causative factor in psychosis, not biology as destiny. Layton (2006, 2017, 2020) has written extensively, juxtaposing relational psychoanalysis with social, political, and cultural processes, seeing the interpenetration and reproduction of structures in all of this. All of this has resulted in expansiveness theoretically in how to think about trauma transmissions.

Notes

1 The Controversial Discussions were a protracted series of meetings of the British Psychoanalytical Society, between October 1942 and February 1944, between the Viennese school, represented by Anna Freud, and the supporters of Melanie Klein.

2 Many changes in theory and technique over the years continue to raise the specter and criticism of not being psychoanalytic, including face-to-face treatment, less frequent sessions, and bringing in issues of race, class, ethnicity, and gender, to name a few.

3 See Laub's (2017) writing on rewatching his mother's Holocaust testimony video and his awareness of his multiple identities and the passage of time.

Legacies From Traumas of Slavery and Attachment Ruptures

Frederick Douglass: Personal Story

I was born in Tuckahoe ... in Talbot county, Maryland. I have no accurate knowledge of my age, never having seen any authentic record containing it. By far the larger part of the slaves know as little of their ages as horses know of theirs, and it is the wish of most masters within my knowledge to keep their slaves thus ignorant ... The white children could tell their ages.

My mother was named Harriet Bailey. She was the daughter of Isaac and Betsey Bailey, both colored, and quite dark. My mother was of a darker complexion than either my grandmother or grandfather. My father was a white man ... The opinion was also whispered that my master was my father; but of the correctness of this opinion, I know nothing; the means of knowing was withheld from me. My mother and I were separated when I was but an infant—before I knew her as my mother. It is a common custom, in the part of Maryland from which I ran away, to part children from their mothers at a very early age. Frequently, before the child has reached its twelfth month, its mother is taken from it ... For what this separation is done, I do not know, unless it be to hinder the development of the child's affection toward its mother, and to blunt and destroy the natural affection of the mother for the child. This is the inevitable result.

I never saw my mother, to know her as such, more than four or five times in my life; and each of these times was very short in duration, and at night. She was hired by a Mr. Stewart, who lived about twelve miles from my home. She made her journeys to see me in the night, travelling the whole distance on foot, after the performance of her day's work. She was a field hand, and a whipping is the penalty of not being in the field at sunrise. I do not recollect

DOI: 10.4324/9781003087762-4

ever seeing my mother by the light of day. She was with me in the night. She would lie down with me, and get me to sleep, but long before I waked she was gone … Death soon ended what little we could have while she lived, and with it her hardships and suffering. She died when I was about seven years old … I was not allowed to be present during her illness, at her death, or burial. She was gone long before I knew anything about it. Never having enjoyed, to any considerable extent, her soothing presence, her tender and watchful care, I received the tidings of her death with much the same emotions I should have probably felt at the death of a stranger.

(Frederick Douglass, excerpt from The life of Frederick Douglas, 1845: pp. 1–2)

Legacies From Slavery
Traumas Enacted, Attachment Ruptures Repaired

Kirkland Vaughans, Ph.D.: Personal Story*

Because of the imperatives of survival, we, Black Americans, have colluded in our own invisibility by shrouding painful and degrading aspects of our past and placing our faith in the future … I recall sixty years ago my father's painful confrontation with the past when a picture of my White maternal great-grandfather arrived in the mail. He violently threw it in the garbage, saying that no picture of a White bastard that had preyed on Black women would ever hang in my house. My White great-grandfather had eighteen children by several different Black women, and their descendants are largely divided by color cleavage to this day. Those who pass as White, and those who are very light, go by his surname of Arbuthnot, and the others, including me, are known as Vaughan. It is only now that I am finally able to reach back into that garbage and reclaim that picture as part of my heritage as a part of my own identity.

A confrontation with my own son challenged my own comforting illusion that I had worked through these issues in my multiple therapies and two personal analyses. The fact of the matter is that the topic of race and the trauma of slavery was never broached in any of these therapies. In chastising my young son David over some misdeed, I asked him, "if he was out of his cotton-picking mind." He responded with the perplexed inquiry, "Dad, why would my mind have to be cotton picking?" Apologized to him and assured him that it was my mind that was still "cotton picking," not his; that some injuries just take an awful long time to heal, especially when we are unaware of our wounds …

(Excerpt from: "To Unchain Haunting Blood Memories;
Intergenerational Trauma among African Americans,"
2017, pp. 235–236)

DOI: 10.4324/9781003087762-5

Note

* Kirkland Vaughans is Professor at the Derner School of Psychology, a
  member of Black Psychoanalysts Speak and co-editor of *The Psychology
  of Black Boys and Adolescents*.

2

Between Silence and Words

Attachment, Trauma, and the Mode of Transgenerational Transmissions

Jill Salberg

In some fundamental way, attachment is the basis for our emotional lives. Feeling attached serves to create an experience of safety and security, allowing us to learn how to be socially human and operationally teaching us how to self-regulate our affective lives. I (Salberg, 2015) have argued that the deep affective attachment unit of parents and children is the vehicle through which trauma is transgenerationally transmitted.

> Children are constantly observing their parents' gestures and affects, absorbing their parents' conscious and unconscious minds. The parent's deep bond and affective intensity may be generated from within an unmetabolized trauma scene. As a consequence, the child—in order to attach to this parent and get this parent attached to her/him— will need to enter and become enmeshed in the trauma scene.
>
> (p. 23)

Attachment has a primal role in our psyches, and trauma can cause massive disruption and disorganization of the parent-child bonding system.

While the parent may at times be reliving aspects of their own trauma, the child lives out, with this parent, a particular attachment dynamic. This specific dynamic may have moments of closeness and safety with other moments of dysregulation, of intense anxiety, or anger or withdrawal. The child will probably have variable attachment security; that is, with certain self-states of their parent/caregivers or with different parents experience more secure attachment, while with other

DOI: 10.4324/9781003087762-6

parent/caregivers feel less securely attached or more disorganized in their attachment. These may become internalized as separate self-states,[1] with each having their distinctive affective mood and possibly differing attachment styles. Somewhere there will be the seeds of attachment rupture, poor repair, and injury. These are the elements of traumatic transmissions from one parent to their child and to the next child/generation.

In this chapter, I will examine attachment theory and its place within psychoanalysis, highlighting the way attachment patterning becomes a primary mode of transgenerational transmission. I will also critique limitations found in the theory and research.

Attachment Theory in Psychoanalysis

The arrival of Bowlby's work (1965, 1973, 1980) was a watershed moment. Before his landmark books on attachment, the preponderant theories in psychoanalysis (which meant Freud and his adherents, such as Melanie Klein) had been predominantly based on drive theory. Psychoanalytic theories outline the progression of these drives throughout childhood development. In drive theory, the primary focus was on the satisfaction or delay of gratification.

It was Bowlby who uniquely understood the traumatic effects of real-life separations from primary caregivers. Bowlby's own remembrance of losing his beloved nanny at age 4 and at age 7 (1914) being sent away to boarding school for education and protection from bombings during World War II proved this to him. He painfully recounted that this shouldn't be forced upon even a dog. During his supervision with Melanie Klein, Bowlby became interested in a mother's extremely anxious state and its impact on the child. Despite Klein's indifference to this, Bowlby forged ahead in exploring the "intergenerational transmission of attachment difficulties and how unresolved issues in one generation can be visited on the next" (Coates, 2004a, p. 577). In the acknowledgments of his first volume, Bowlby (1965) wrote, "For my psychoanalytic education I am indebted especially to my own analyst, Joan Riviere, and to Melanie Klein, who was one of my supervisors" (p. xxxiii). Nonetheless, a deep rift ensued. By volume 2 there are no psychoanalysts in the acknowledgments, but instead Mary Ainsworth appears, whose work with Bowlby in the UK and later development of the Strange Situation research protocol allowed for attachment research to validate his findings and elaborate his work more fully. Had Bowlby's work been accepted into psychoanalysis, there would have been a fertile interpenetration of ideas.

Instead, the British Psychoanalytical Society alienated Bowlby, view-ing his ideas as non-psychoanalytic.

It is likely that Bowlby's rift with Klein was seen as a betrayal not only of Klein's ideas, but also of the entire psychoanalytic enterprise. Klein was dedicated to expanding Freud's intrapsychic developmen-tal vision to early infancy, the pre-oedipal years. It is interesting to note that Klein's alignment with Freud—specifically, the adherence to the death instinct and the privileging of internal phantasy over real-ity/trauma—was antithetical to the view of her first analyst, Ferenczi. However, her persistent disinterest in the actual mother and the real environment were in direct opposition to Bowlby's experiences during the war years, when he helped evacuate children out of London.

Bowlby believed it was misguided to focus exclusively on internal phantasy without regard for the *actual* mother. Despite the lack of sup-port from the British Society—Holmes (1996) suggests that Bowlby was "virtually airbrushed out of the psychoanalytic record—rather like some dissident in Stalinist times" (p. 20)—Bowlby maintained that his work on attachment as a primary motivational system was indeed deeply psychoanalytic.

So, what exactly made Bowlby so heretical? First, Bowlby asserted that another drive was essential in psychoanalysis—a motivational sys-tem based on attachment. He diminished the reliance on sexual and ag-gressive drives as explanatory of human behavior. Second, he argued that real events, the real mother, and mother-child interaction are cru-cial in development. This placed him in the company of Ferenczi and Fairbairn, also outliers in the psychoanalytic canon. His concept of the *internal working model* draws upon object relations theory and ethol-ogy. Bowlby believed that the patterns of attachment between mother/ caregivers and their children are internalized as patterns of relational attachment; this would later be picked up by Stephen Mitchell and the Relational school, expanding psychoanalysis to include interpersonal re-lations, object relations theories, and understandings of trauma models.

Attachment, Trauma, and Transmissions

I will now unpack how a child inevitably becomes intertwined with, and then comes to bear and live out, the family's trauma legacy. Bowlby's (1965) original work on attachment and the subsequent literature have long shown the primary need for children to have a safe base in order to establish secure attachment and how this underlies later social develop-ment. However, if a parent has self-states that are dysregulated or even dissociative, we can assume that they will be in some way emotionally compromised and thus at times inaccessible to the child to help with self-regulation, self-soothing, and mentalization of feelings and thoughts.

The considerable research literature of Ainsworth (1982), Main (1995), and Main and Hesse (1990) greatly expanded Bowlby's concepts. They observed and theorized about children's attachment strategies and styles with their caregivers. Ainsworth wrote about three main strategies that children demonstrate in her "Strange Situation," in which the mother or caregiver leaves their child in a playroom with a "stranger" and then returns after a brief time. How the child handles the reunion with the mother/caregiver is observed and repeated three times to form a sense of a consistent pattern. The three attachment styles—secure, insecure avoidant, and insecure ambivalent—were further expanded by Main, adding a disorganized style. The child who manifests disorganization upon the mother's return reflects a difficulty in establishing an effective strategy for being soothed. These mother/caregivers were found (on interview data and the AAI) to have had difficulties in attaching to their own mothers, and so an intergenerational pattern of attachment styles was being documented. This was true for secure and insecurely attached mothers/caregivers as well. Main and Hesse (1990) argued that their research findings reflected a strong relationship between caregivers' unresolved losses or traumas in their early life and the disorganization of early attachment in their children.

The work of Beebe et al. (2003) and Beebe and Lachmann (2014) focus on mother's difficulty in empathizing with their child's distress. Beebe's research on mother–infant interactions at 4 months old has been predictive of future securely attached and disorganized attachment in 12-month-old and older children.

> As we proposed … future disorganized infants at 4 months cannot develop an expectation of feeling "sense" or "known," particularly when distressed … In attention, the infant may feel not seen; in emotion the infant may feel not joined, and stonewalled when distressed; in orientation the infant experiences looming impingements … At times these infants may feel alarmed or threatened … We hypothesize that dissociative experiences during times of distress later in life have their origins in experiences in infancy of not being sensed, met, known, and recognized, particularly in moments of distress.
>
> (pp. 62–63)

Tronick (1989, 2017) also speaks to maternal distress/depression and the impact of this on the child. His work on the "still face"[2] demonstrates the profound effects on children of maternal depression and dissociation.

Further and equally important to note is a finding by Liotti (2004) in reviewing extensively the research literature:

> These studies, and others following Main and Hesse's original ob-servations (Hesse & Main, 2000; Hesse et al., 2003), provide many disquieting examples of how a parent's state of mind, unresolved as to traumas, may interfere in the communication between parent and child. It is noteworthy that parents' unresolved states of mind can induce fright without solution and dissociative reactions in the infant *even when the parents' behavior does not obviously consti-tute maltreatment.*
>
> (p. 478)

Liotti suggests that other attachment figures capable of providing posi-tive attachment experiences will offer a corrective balance to the dis-organizing attachment experiences within the child. Additionally, he highlights that there is an important difference between the harmful impact of trauma inflicted by an attachment figure and trauma resulting from what he calls an anonymous destructive force.

Written earlier than these attachment research findings, Fraiberg, Adelson, and Shapiro (1975) described what we now would term trauma transmission in these attachment relationships. They identified cases that included multi-generational trauma histories with dysregulated affect and problematic mother-infant attachments. In what reads as a description of a kind of early parent–infant treatment of transgenerational attachment trauma, they offered the traumatized parent a deeply empathic witnessing therapist. In their case of "Mary," we learn of a profoundly depressed and rejecting mother who wants to give up her baby for adoption.

> Mary begins to cry. It is a hoarse, eerie cry in a baby … On tape we see the baby in her mother's arms screaming hopelessly; she does not turn to her mother for comfort. The mother looks distant, self-absorbed. She makes an absent gesture to comfort the baby, then gives up. She looks away … As we watched this tape later in a staff session, we said to each other incredulously, "It's as if this mother doesn't *hear* her baby's cries!"
>
> (p. 392)

The focus of the work was mother–infant treatment in the home. The therapist learns that the mother's own mother had a serious post-partum depression and, in an attempt to kill herself, shot and permanently damaged her face/head and was hospitalized. Mary's mother was subsequently raised by a loving Aunt until age 4/5 and then sent to live with a grandmother who grudgingly raised her. Thus, as a child, Mary felt herself to be unwanted and unlovable. As the therapeutic work helped her to feel empathically held in mind, she spoke of the many traumas, abandonments, and abuses of her childhood. Empathy from the therapist may have been her first experience of witnessing and care. Further, we believe this therapy was interrupting trauma transmissions, allowing her to be held in mind and cared about. This then allowed empathy toward her own child to develop. What Fraiberg et al. documented was how this approach allowed the parent/patient to slowly come out of dissociation and begin to experience pain, grief, and terror for the first time. Slowly, these mothers/caregivers were able to comfort their babies and learn to provide responsive soothing and more secure attachment.

When a parent has experienced trauma, I believe that some part of their mind has been affected and thus may make part of the parent inaccessible to the child. Furthermore, what was demonstrated by Fraiberg et al. was how empathic witnessing intervened and altered transgenerational transmission of attachment trauma, allowing for resilience to be fostered in the mothers. This is crucial, given that research has shown that parents with unresolved traumas have limited capacity to provide consistent and positive experiences with their children. This in turn leads to disorganized attachment behavior in children, whose fearful approach or avoidant responses closely resemble dissociation (see Hesse et al., 2003; Liotti, 2004). Research continues to demonstrate that unresolved trauma carries a crisis in one generation and is transmitted into later generations.

Contemporary Attachment and Neuroscience

Daniel N. Stern (1985) believed that babies' brains were wired for intersubjectivity and that not only were they influenced by their mothers, it was also a mutual influencing relationship. He felt that mothers not only model affects, like a mirroring effect to their infants, but also modulate, what Stern called "theme-and-variation." His work with

Beatrice Beebe looked at micro-analyses of videotaped mother–infant interactions, documenting dynamics and precursors of attachment, both secure and insecure (D.N. Stern et al., 1975; Beebe et al., 2003). Stern wrote about maternal attunement wherein the mother not only imitates but resonates with the affective state of her infant. Many see this as a precursor to the concept of emotional regulation that has grown out of neuroscience research.

The work of Peter Fonagy (1999a) provides a kind of theoretical through-line from Bowlby and Anna Freud to contemporary psycho-analytic attachment theory and research, to Daniel Stern, to Jay Green-berg and Stephen Mitchell. In his collaborative book (Fonagy et al., 2005), we have a new iteration of attachment theory and research find-ings. Fonagy weaves these into psychoanalytic developmental theory, forming a new psychoanalytic concept of self-reflective function and mentalization, defining mentalization as the ability to read other peo-ple's emotional states, seeing this as a crucial part of psyche-social development. The caregiver's mind forms knowledge of their baby's emotional state; this is internally represented and then projected into the child in attuned emotional responses. The failure to do this, be-cause of the mother's limitations, prevents the child from developing beyond what they termed *psychic equivalence*, a primitive mindset in which there is no distinction between one's thoughts and what is in the world. As the child moves from psychic equivalence to mentaliza-tion, the child will develop the ability to cognitively represent its own and other's mental states. This capacity becomes part of self-reflective functioning necessary to have a sense of oneself and of others. These ideas are rooted in attachment theory and Bowlby's IWM as well as Stern's concept of attunement.

Alan Schore (2001, 2003a, 2003b) advanced the field with his re-search work on brain development and his scholarly integration of Bowlby's work on the attachment motivation system and the research it fostered. Schore argues that Bowlby's work was groundbreaking in that he was attempting to integrate a science of psychobiological mechanisms with the psychological, suggesting that it was a fuller elaboration of Freud's attempt to integrate neurology and psychology.

The findings from neuroscience continue to support many of Bowl-by's original ideas. Specifically, Schore's (2003a) research has found that the development of the brain (specifically right brain development from 7 to 15 months) occurs in synchronicity between the infant and the mother/caregiver, whose attunement helps to regulate the infant's positive and negative states. As a result, the infant is "forming internal working models of the attachment relationship [that] are processed and stored in implicit-procedural memory systems in the right hemisphere" (p. 64). These models are the ways that infants begin to develop their sense of self with others, how their emotions will be reacted to, and therefore how to self-regulate. The maintenance of attachment to mother/caregiver is always primary even when problematic: As one patient once quipped to me in session, "Even a bad mother is better than no mother." Further research has substantiated that regulation of emotion is central to self-regulation, the ability to flexibly regulate emotional states through interactions with other humans—interactive regulation in interconnected contexts, and without other humans—autoregulation in autonomous contexts: "The adaptive capacity to shift between these dual regulatory modes … emerges out of a history of secure attachment interactions of a maturing biological organism and an early attuned social environment" (Schore, 2003a, pp. 63–64).

The more secure our attachment, the more flexibly we learn how to move through our feelings and calm ourselves when stressed. The obverse is also true, and as the research literature has grown, so has our understanding of the extensive issues and problems that follow from children who—because of poor attunement, neglect, or abuse—are disorganized in their attachment. These experiences often are not one-time events, but ongoing and chronic, resulting in ruptured attachments and disorganized attachment dynamics—the essence of relational trauma.

Recent and critical in the research literature is the burgeoning field of epigenetics, specifically the study of maternal stress measured by hormones and cortisol levels during pregnancy. Neuroscience suggests that epigenetics may account for some of the findings of transgenerational transmission of stress as measured by increased cortisol levels. Kohler (2012), in summarizing research findings on the effects of environment on epigenetics, writes:

> Some epigenetic "marks," i.e., specific chemical attachments such as a methyl group, can be trans-generationally transmitted … In the context where epigenetic changes can be inherited and passed on to subsequent generations, the "nurture" of one generation contributes to the "nature" of subsequent generations.

The fuller legacy of transgenerational transmission of traumatic forms of attachment reveals an alteration in both the biology and the attachment systems. The epigenetic research increasingly points to clear biological changes related to levels of PTSD in parents that have also been found to be transmitted to children of survivors of trauma. The biological markers of trauma as seen in cortisol levels, receptor site alterations, and myelinization changes are found to affect gene expression and are inheritable by the next generation. Some of these children are inherently more anxious while being raised by parents surviving their own traumas.

My understanding of this is that children inherit altered biochemistry that can leave them more vulnerable to registering fearful and anxious situations and to being more fearful and anxious themselves.[3] Traumatized caregivers are raising children with greater propensities for fear. These studies reflect the more advanced understanding of how changes resulting from extreme traumatization may in fact be transferred from parent to child. Thus, it becomes very evident that in order to understand the capacity and, what I have termed the *texture* of attachment, we must consider biology along with the psycho-emotional development of both the child and the caregivers.

Contemporary Relational Interpersonal Theory, Attachment, and Trauma

The foundations for what has become known as Relational psychoanalysis or the "relational turn" in psychoanalysis were multiple. Contemporary Relational theory drew on Ferenczi's rediscovered papers along with the translation of his *Clinical Diary* into English, object relations theory, interpersonal theory, self-psychology, and attachment theory and research. The relational turn was one that, as Stephen Mitchell argued, would link disparate theories and theorists who put human relationality at the forefront, such as Bowlby, Fairbairn, Loewald, Sullivan, and Winnicott.[4] Mitchell (1999) believed that relational psychoanalysis was a new bridge between their work and the intrapsychic drive-based classical model.

> Bowlby always seemed to have regarded the choice between privileging "real events" versus "fantasy" as a key fork in the road separating attachment theory from psychoanalysis … Some of the more innovative psychoanalytic theorizing, these days, links fantasy not with drives but with imagination. In this view, developed by Loewald and Winnicott, reality is encountered, inevitably, through imagination and fantasy.
>
> (p. 93)

At the same time, a dynamic and interesting collegial relationship developed between Phillip Bromberg and Alan Schore, both working on aspects of developmental affect theory. Bromberg focused on the development of a sense of self and the effects of dissociation and interpersonal conflict. Schore, from a developmental neuroscience interest in right brain development, suggests that the relationship between infant and caregiver impacts emotional regulation. Schore termed his approach an interpersonal neurobiological model of attachment.

The dissociative model of the mind dates back to the early work of Janet (see Chapter 1) but was elaborated by Relational and Interpersonal theorists such as Jody Davies, Adrienne Harris, Phillip Bromberg, Elizabeth Howell, Shelley Itzkowitz, and others. Bromberg has argued that during intense stress and relational discord, dissociative aspects of mind become drafted and then utilized in a direct defensive capacity. Bromberg (2006) writes,

> the normal function of dissociation is enlisted as a defense against trauma, the brain uses dissociation to inhibit potentially discrepant views of reality held by different self-states, which, if "on stage" at the same time, would be more than the mind could contain without destabilizing.

> (p. 4)

Further, he maintains that this creates deep divisions in the mind between what different self-states know, feel, and experience and emotional capacities.

Similarly, Clara Mucci (2022) believes it is important to distinguish the levels of interpersonal traumatization as follows: 1) misattunement between mother and infant/child (what has been called early relational trauma by Bromberg and Schore); 2) active abuse or mistreatment of child by adults (parent, caregiver, or relative, which is the original contribution of Ferenczi); and 3) collective and massive traumatizations such as war, political mass torture, and genocide. She views attachment, in a similar vein to Bromberg, Schore, and Salberg, as the key mediator in trauma experience.

> The attachment system works as a buffer (in the case of secure attachment) or as an amplifier of the stress. In other words, the person who has experienced trauma of the first or second level will react with more stress, more anxiety, more neurobiological disruption to

the further traumatizations of human origin, or of natural or accidental origin.

(p. 72)

Mucci argues, drawing further upon the work of Tronick (2017) and others, that attachment is pivotal to understanding the impact of trauma. Emotional/psychological development is all dyadic, meaning it does not happen only inside of the child but occurs in the context of the caretaking relationship.

Attachment as Key Mode of Trauma Transmissions

Predating and concurrent with Bowlby's development of attachment theory in England was the work being done in the United States by Henry Stack Sullivan (1953), whose interest in cultural forces and the immediate interpersonal interaction held far more interest for him than Freud's ideas on the intrapsychic. Sullivan, like Bowlby, was focused on the infant and the environment he/she grew up within, seeing the interactions between child and mother as formative. The toxic effect of the mother's anxiety on the child was critical in the development of Sullivan's ideas about defensive operations—specifically, personifications of *good-me*, *not-me*, and *bad-me*. Although not a direct theory of multiple self-states or an explicit study of attachment, this conception of Sullivan's is a clear precursor to what we now call *relational trauma*.

Dori Laub's testimonial work with Holocaust survivors contributed greatly to our understanding of the transgenerational transmission of trauma. His metaphor of *the empty circle* (see Chapter 1) affectingly captures the oddness of these traumatic transmissions in the context of the parent–child attachment relationship. There is a puzzling contradiction here of absence—of a gap of knowledge—and of emptiness, simultaneously mixed with over-fullness or an excess of certain affects: often fear, dread, and even terror. It is the rupture of either a real empathic dyadic experience or a fantasied one that had already been internalized that becomes destroyed.

What are the affective aspects and psychic consequences for the child of an emotionally absent or fragmented parent? Andre Green (1972) was the first to describe this kind of absent parent whom he termed a *dead mother*—someone alive but not present, once enlivened but now, due to depression, lost to the child in what must seem an inexplicable way. This state of blankness causes the child's premature disillusionment with the mother. In detaching from this *dead mother* while simultaneously identifying with her, Green believed that deadness and loss of meaning are installed in the unconscious psyche. Green terms this a *psychosis blanche*—a blank or white state, absent anxiety or mourning.

I have wondered what has befallen a deadened mother and caused such deep despair? And in the presence of this deadened state, what happens inside of the child? This sounds like a moment of trauma transmission: The caregiver may be reliving moments of trauma, and the child experiences an aspect of the trauma that the parent has been unable to metabolize. What is clear is that children are hungry for emotional/psychological contact with their parents, whether this is conceptualized as a search for safety (Bowlby, e.g., 1965, or an attachment imperative, Bromberg, 2011).

I believe that the child will seek out even the parent's traumatized self. In the absence of an emotionally vital and present parent, the child attaches not only to what is present, but also to what is absent—what is alive as well as what is deadened (Salberg, 2015). This is Gerson's (2009) significant contribution: helping us understand that the imprint of absence on the child, the legacy of the trauma and loss without someone to empathically witness these experiences, becomes what he termed—referencing Green (1972)—a *dead third*. He noted that the final experience for such a child is a "not-there-ness [that] constitutes both the 'gap' or absence as well as what fills the absence" (p. 1347).

Schore (2001) and Fonagy (1999a, 1999b) have written at great length regarding the necessary function that caregivers provide to the emotional and cognitive growth of children. When the parent/caregiver suffers from unmetabolized traumatic experience, their child cannot emotionally feel held or attuned to this parent. What might a child have to do to attach to the parent? Grand (2000) saw this as the child's craving to connect to the absent space in the traumatized parent, describing the resultant holes in parental bonding. The second generation's search for the parents' traumatized and pre-traumatized selves she describes as: "To search for one's parent and to find fear in a handful of dust: such a dilemma precipitates a hunger for visceral contact with the parent's traumatized self" (pp. 25–26).

How does this child attach and feel connected to the parent who has had to detach from his or her own experience and mind? I (2015) proposed that the knowledge gained from attachment theory and infant research (e.g., Beebe & Lachmann, 2014; Coates, 2004a, 2004b, 2012, 2016; Lyons-Ruth, 2002, 2003; Slade, 2014) and the new emphasis on empathic attunement (Bruschweiler-Stern et al., 2010), as well as work on relational trauma (Bromberg, 2006, 2011; Schore, 2001), explains the child's necessary engagement and internalization of their parent's trauma experience. Absence, deadness, and dysregulated attachment are common features of survival (Bergmann & Jucovy, 1982; Davoine & Gaudillière, 2004; Faimberg, 1996, 1998, 2005; Gampel, 2019; Grand, 2000; Laub, 1995). We can now apprehend the dilemma of second and third generations who, from birth, have been cared for by parents with dysregulated affects and possibly dissociative self-states.

Contemporary Theories and Research: Relational Trauma

As a result of the unmetabolized trauma of actual events, attachment is inevitably affected, and what we have come to call *relational trauma* or *complex relational trauma* ensues (Coates, 2004a, 2004b, 2012; Fonagy, 1999b; Mucci, 2022). In their primary attachment relationships, these children have had to manage fragmentation resulting from parental traumatization. Schore (2001) states,

> During episodes of the intergenerational transmission of attachment trauma the infant is matching the rhythmic structures of the mother's dysregulated arousal states … This growth-inhibiting relational environment is a context for the real-time intergenerational transmission of an enduring susceptibility to attachment trauma and to the unconscious use of a dissociative defense against overwhelming and dysregulating affective states.
>
> (p. xix)

The caveat here is that this is not true of *all* such children, since survival resilience can also be transmitted and, as Liotti (2004) found, significant others in the child's life can provide more secure attachment experiences.

Slade (2014) argues that we need to rediscover Bowlby's clear emphasis on *fear* as the motivational basis for attachment and a significant factor in the organization of psychic experience. This is key to understanding the biological underpinnings that Bowlby tried to integrate with psychic experience. When caregivers fail to soothe or are abandoning or are frightening, the child's attachment suffers. Slade urges us to keep in mind that since fear is so primal in our evolutionary biological/social being, anything that increases fear is problematic. Trauma clearly complicates attachment, and when it is transmitted transgenerationally, the person of safety may also be the person to be feared. Lieberman (2014) underscores this, writing:

> Dysregulated and traumatized parents can be very frightening to their children ... They transmit their internal disorganization to their children, not only by directing their anger, punitiveness, and unpredictability towards the child but also by exposing them to a cacophony of daily, real-life situations that are helplessly witnessed or experienced by the child.
>
> (p. 278)

Harris (2014) incorporates Slade's underscoring of fear in attachment with Bromberg's elaboration of dissociative self-states: "The intergenerational transmission of trauma in which fear states linked often to unrecognized experiences of disrupted safety in one generation leak into and terrorize the next, often in nonverbal and early unmetabolized forms" (p. 270). When the traumatized parent remains resilient and alive, this state shifting or fragmentation may be tolerable and fleeting for the child. I have argued that in order to bond and attach in ever-more dysregulated circumstances, the child must attune to implicit communications about the trauma story. The child must do this in order to have an attachment relationship, thereby becoming attached to a parent's presence and absence.

The matching and tuning "dance" done by the child is often what attachment researchers like Lyons-Ruth (2002, 2003) consider a form of role reversal—that is, the child is attempting to affectively regulate the parent in lieu of the parent regulating the child. This is the child's ongoing attempt to repair the parent from the outside—a repair that can never be complete since the damage is actually on the inside. This will become what I have termed

> the *texture of traumatic attachment*—how it feels to this child to feel connected to the parent. This textured affective experience is one in which the child shapes him-/herself to fit a parent's wound of history, be it war, rape, slavery, death—the list goes on. This may

also be the place in which the child grows a kind of resilience, since in role reversal, the child is called upon to grow up sooner and to be, in a precocious manner, the more affectively regulated one.

(Salberg, 2015, p. 35)

The parent's deep bond and affective intensity may be generated from within an unmetabolized trauma scene. Therefore, the child—in order to attach to this parent and get this parent attached to her/him—will need to enter and become enmeshed in the trauma scene. Through empathic mirroring and what Hopenwasser (2008) called *dissociative attunement*, the parents' trauma story enters the child's cellular makeup preverbally, and thus before a narrative. Harris (2006), in writing about ghosts, captures the haunting quality of these transgenerational transmissions and believes that ghosts exist where mourning has been foreclosed.

What I maintain is that attachment functions as the mode of transmission in most transgenerational transmissions. In this way, enacting trauma is less a discrete event and becomes what is referred to as relational trauma. I believe that transgenerational transmission is not so much a clear transmission of something, either content or experience, but sequelae of a traumatized person's fragmented states of mind. It is the dysregulated affect states of the parent that infuse the child's attachment experience and evoke fantasies of the parent's missing stories. There are often missing pieces of the trauma: Sometimes it is the narrative, sometimes the affect, and sometimes both. This is where trauma meets attachment theories.

The child needs to feel that they have access to and can live inside the mind of the parent. I have had patients who, in order to maintain their bond with a depressed or anxious mother, had to become the mother's caretaker. One patient knew that if she could calm her mother by stroking her arm or hair, then she had some chance of deriving some mothering from her. Further, I have argued that if part of that mind is deadened, hidden, and/or dissociated, the search for the parent becomes dire. In many ways, it is a search for a missing bond, an attachment to an absence (Gerson, 2009; Grand, 2000). How much do they have to, in Lyon-Ruth's (2002, 2003) vernacular, enter a role reversal and emotionally regulate and "parent/take care of" their parent?

Reis (2009, 2015),[5] in writing about trauma and witnessing, believes that what is described in the clinical cases and theories in the transgenerational transmission literature is much the same as what is found when caregivers have unresolved mourning or trauma (non-Holocaust related). Drawing upon Fonagy, Holmes, and the work of Lyons-Ruth on disorganized attachment, Reis concludes that it is not trauma but the fragmented mental state of the caregiver that is transmitted via the attachment relationship that becomes problematic.

Evidence of these complex multi-generational transmissions can be seen in the work of Schechter (2003, 2017), who has researched and documented post-traumatic stress in parental histories. He found that, inevitably, these mothers' emotional regulation becomes self-directed: "PTSD is a disorder of emotion dysregulation in which traumatic memory traces and their associated affects overwhelm the individual such that their priority must turn to survival and self-regulation rather than affiliation and mutual regulation" (2017, p. 265). In his research, he has observed that the mother's PTSD state triggers alarm in the child without any link to an actual fearful situation. The child and mother are experientially in a new traumatizing dynamic: "the child and mother are left with a new traumatic experience that they share and have co-constructed that nevertheless transmits 'the traumatic' essence in part at least of mother's prior experience" (p. 267).

Problematizing the Attachment Literature

It remains important to critique this generative literature. First, it is important to notice that, for most of the authors cited above, critical attachment functions are attributed to the *mother*. At times, this language shifts to "caregiver," "parental object," or "maternal function." However, this literature is still suffering from cultural biases that presume these functions are the exclusive responsibility of female bodies. Insofar as this responsibility adheres to female, domesticated bodies, female bodies must *also* bear the burden of guilt if these functions go awry in family or in culture. Generally, we hear nothing of fathers, as fathers are presumed to be out in the world working, while the work of mentalization is proceeding at home. In psychoanalysis, fathers are usually written into the child's psyche as the *third* in an oedipal triangle.

This construction borrows upon, and sustains, traditional sex roles; it presumes a middle-class, Western, nuclear family structure; it erases other gendered and familial arrangements. In contemporary times, we can certainly recognize that the "mother" in the family may have a penis, not a vagina. We can recognize, as Benjamin (1988) put it, the need for a *subjective* mother. Nonetheless, as Grand (2019) has written, the familial construct at the heart of psychoanalytic theory—mommy, daddy, baby—remains problematic. It burdens *one domestic* figure with the role of mentalization; it excuses all others from that provision. To Grand, this can actually *deplete* the maternal function that we valorize as the conduit to trauma healing. In her view, it is no surprise then, that we focus on "dead mothers," ruptured attachment, and failures in mentalization as the sequelae of trauma. Grand argues that, like traditional Western culture, psychoanalysis has constructed an idealized and *overburdened* Mother. Insofar as we use this lens to look at trauma survival and its transmissions, we might become fixated in the "pathological tilt" described by Richman (2017).

Grand contends that we have no theoretical infrastructure with which to theorize the *strengths* of survival. After atrocity, survivors do not simply develop an *empty circle*. As Richman (2018), Ornstein (2003, 2004), Stoute (2019, 2021), and others note, survivors transmit strengths and an enduring capacity to love. When the traumatized parent remains resilient and alive, their injured states may be tolerable and fleeting for the child. The transmission of the trauma does not just take the shape of filling a parental absence; it becomes a venue for ethics, empathy, pride, and resiliency.

In summary, attachment is a pivotal and crucial dimension in mediating and surviving trauma, which is in many cases transmitted to the next generation. It is well documented in the literature how transmissions of traumatic experiences from mother/caregiver to child become reproduced in that relationship. It is crucial to note that side by side with traumatizing transmissions are also aspects of resilience. It is a complexity that should not be reduced in our minds to simply victim or perpetrator. Additionally, the role of significant others, be it the other parent/caregiver, grandparents, extended family, or nanny/babysitters, can offset these transmissions. The child's capacity to internalize more than one figure and more than one way of attaching should not be overlooked. Nor should we forget that early intervention through the schools' efforts or treatment can help these families heal and restore capacities toward resilience and growth.

Notes

1 This is in line with Bromberg's (2011) work on self-states as response to trauma.
2 For Tronick's discussion and demonstration, see www.youtube.com/watch?v=f1Jw0-LExyc.

3 See the work of Bowers and Yehuda (2016) and Yehuda et al. (2015) on Holocaust intergenerational transmissions and Perroud et al. (2014) on the Tutsi genocide and transgenerational transmission of maternal stress and others.

4 See Mitchell (1999) for his understanding of how these theorists developed their relational core ideas and how they ended up on the margins of psychoanalytic theory until after their death.

5 Reis has been writing from an interesting intersection of analytic theories of subjectivity, infant research (as part of the BCPSG), and intersubjective perspectives.

3

The Wound and Its Social Imperatives

Sue Grand

> Somewhere, far away, another cry mourns toward me, another
> which is the same, the same cry uttered, sung by another voice. As
> the reply ends, a certitude … comes to me that now it has happened.
> Nothing more. Just this, and in this way—now it has happened …
> that happening which gave rise to my cry has only now, with the
> rejoinder, really and undoubtedly happened.
>
> (Buber, 1923, pp. 1–2)

Transgenerational processes have been cast as an effort to bond to, represent, and repair the unmetabolized history of our forebears. Succeeding generations are implicitly called to a *witnessing function*, a term derived from Holocaust studies (see Laub & Auerhahn, 1993). This is a relational process: The survivor's testimony calls for an empathic other who can receive this testimony. Traumatic events are assumed to produce some deficit in the mentalizing "maternal function"; the witness offers its reparative provision.

The *developmental* foundations of witnessing reflect those of ordinary childhood, even as *witnessing* inscribes experiences that radically depart from the human. Being-in-relation with the *benign authority* of early caregivers facilitates agency and self-knowing. Our evolving self-story is rooted in both psyche and soma; it has conscious and unconscious features; it incorporates self-other imagoes; it is sensory, preverbal, *and* symbolic. All of this is infused with, and inseparable from, culture. This object-relational process allows us to seek the comfort of others; we enhance our resiliency and reflectivity. We can feel generative guilt and "creative shame" in relation to the injured other (see Grand, 2018a). This yields an ethical orientation. To birth this

DOI: 10.4324/9781003087762-7

vitalized and humane soul, familial responsiveness needs to be embedded in *cultural* responsiveness.

It is understood that the *familial* environment is always imperfect. In the social-ethical turn of psychoanalysis, it is *also* understood that *cultural responsiveness* is deeply flawed. Our self-narrative is shaped by the flaws, breaks, edicts, prescriptions, and prohibitions in the familial/cultural environment, as well as by the repairs in that environment. In our clinical/cultural work, we are interested in the *gaps* in responsiveness/repair throughout our lives (see Layton, 2020). All of this is linked to how psychoanalysis views humanity in times of extremis. When individuals and groups are subjugated by malignant forces, they are often met by the silence of an unresponsive world. From a developmental framework, this unresponsiveness appears as a deficit in the containing "maternal function."

Healing, then, is a multilayered process, requiring empathic recognition for a wound that has had none. We cannot underscore this enough. The failure of recognition by the interpersonal and cultural worlds is catastrophic. As we discussed earlier, we cannot live in a world without attachments. Objectless-ness is an impossible condition. With trauma of this magnitude, recognition needs to occur in inter-subjective *and* cultural contexts, in intimate spaces *and* in public inscriptions. Within psychoanalytic dyads, witnessing becomes a crucial healing process because of its two-person form. This intersubjective inscription hopes to answer the inchoate pain of trauma, releasing its subject. The term *traumatic witnessing* also echoes the legal terminology of *witnessing*, which refers to the giving of *testimony in a court of law, particularly in reference to a crime that has occurred.* Testimony to past crimes and the need for a public transcript in a lawful world: Witnessing is an *ethical* act; it is inseparable from social justice.

The Wound: Narrative Holes and Epistemic Erasures

This chapter reviews theories of witnessing and provides illustrations. Let's begin with a question that seems to have an obvious answer: *What* are we witnessing? The obvious answer is: Whatever descendants of survivors *need* us to witness. Witnessing is an other-centered project. It is not for us to predetermine the focus of our empathic response; as Orange (2011) and Goodman (2012) suggest, we need to answer the call of the Other. When the original Holocaust literature formulated the relation between the wounded and the witness, it was answering this call. The resultant concepts have been applied to malignant trauma, around the world.

Nonetheless, the portrait of witnessing produced by Holocaust studies has its biases and limitations, which will be elucidated in this chapter. One obvious problem has been observed by Gentile (2017): Rooted in post-Holocaust studies, *witnessing* tends to assume that the trauma is temporally discrete, located in the past, with its survivors (and their descendants) largely situated in a much more secure present. This relatively secure present has been assumed to be the platform in which descendants can inherit, and reflect upon, *past* trauma. This fits the temporality of the Holocaust. But, as Gentile points out, for many individuals and groups, malignant trauma is never *past*; rather, the persecutory practices of the past just morph into new, ongoing forms. There is no safe, contemporary platform from which to examine historical wounds. This has implications for witnessing. I will return to these cultural critiques, but first, I will examine the original formulation of Holocaust studies.

Narrative Holes

How do we turn past events into events of the past that can be mourned? The original Holocaust literature focused on restoring traumatic knowledge to the survivor's self-narrative. For Laub, the survivor *cannot, themselves*, narrate the events of their history *without an empathic witness*. Without that witness, traumatic events remain timeless, suspended in dissociative gaps, inchoate states, and repetitions. For Laub (1992) and his colleagues (Laub & Auerhahn, 1993; Laub & Podell, 1995), trauma is defined by conditions that exceed linguistic knowing, so that traumatic events preclude their own registration in the mind. From this perspective, traumatic events become *knowable* to their subject *only* as the testimony is heard and received by an empathic other. To paraphrase Laub, malignant trauma is an "event without a witness," making it unknowable to its subject. Caruth (1995) evokes this predicament when she states that "the force of this (traumatic) experience would appear to arise precisely … in the collapse of its understanding" (p. 7). This view is consonant with that of Baranger, Baranger, and Mom (1998), who declare that "We can think of the subject of 'pure trauma' as a subject without a history" (p. 69).

This assumption—that malignant trauma vacates the mind of its own traumatic knowledge—was linked to a view of traumatized states in which the internal, mentalizing "mother" is rendered vacant, dead, or frozen. This speechlessness of the (real, or internal) "mother" is evoked by French analyst Altounian (1999), a daughter of a survivor of the Armenian genocide:

> Every child of emigrants who have survived an extermination is surely charged with ... restoring life and meaning to the traces handed down to her by her parents ... the paradoxical, tragic message that cannot be put into words between the mother, the environment and the child of this history is something like its own negation: "We are transmitting to you a life without symbolic reference."
>
> (pp. 441–442)

Even though she was the recipient of her father's diary of the genocide; even though she was inspired and held by *real* parental presence, Altounian evokes the evisceration of the inner "protective parental shield" (Grand, 2000). In particular, she points to the *lack* of public, historic recognition of the Armenian genocide. Descendants of the Armenian genocide have struggled to gain international recognition for this crime (see Hachikian, 2017). This lack differentiates her heritage from that of descendants of Holocaust survivors. Altounian (1999) asks: "How can the unthinkable content of this *secret* crime inhabit the psyche?" (p. 443).

As discussed previously, Holocaust studies proposed that the maternal function can become a *dead mother* (Green, 1972) in the aftermath of an atrocity. We have queried this over-generalization. Here, I focus on the underlying assumptions about traumatic knowing. The Holocaust literature proposes that extreme events vacate the survivor's mind of its own narrative. If the mentalizing function is essential to self-knowing; if the mentalizing function has turned into a *dead mother*, what can be left of the knowing subject? For Laub and Auerhahn (1993) and for Felman (1995), Grand (2000), Caruth (1995), and Langer (1991), this collapse would yield a state in which "there is no knower and there is no known; one's very mind has been evacuated of its own defining moment ... Victimization is a relation defined by its intersubjective lapse, by its failure of human intercourse" (Grand, 2000, p. 24).

Laub and Podell (1995) describe this as an *empty circle* at the epicenter of self and memory. As previously noted, this *empty circle* is akin to Green's (1972) blank psychosis, to Grotstein's (1990) "black hole of nothingness," to the remoteness of Guntrip's (1969) schizoid inner core, and it is linked to Gerson's (2009) *dead third*. This is an area of objectless-ness that is filled up with persecutory objects. Unknown and unknowable, *the empty circle* is inchoate, speechless, empty, and deadened; it is vacated of its own traumatic knowledge. For Grand (2000), *the empty circle* is a site of "catastrophic loneliness" in which there is the "imperative to tell, and the impossibility of telling" (p. 35). This loneliness inscribes that radical human absence in which there was no I–Thou.

This literature is often written in a tone which is definitive, unfortunately pathologizing traumatized interiority. As we have noted, this literature has been aptly criticized by both Richman (2017, 2020) and Anna Ornstein (2003). The retention of an internal self-witness is an example of that resiliency which Ornstein underscores in survivors. It seems difficult for us to recognize both the *wounds* inflicted *and* the human strengths that endure through trauma. Reflecting on this conundrum, Grand (2009) suggests that we have difficulty addressing both the wound and the strengths of survival.

Nonetheless, this sense that atrocity vacates its own narrative certainly resonates with many clinicians, survivors, and their descendants. Working in Argentina and Peru to heal the trauma of political torture and disappearance, Varea (2011) writes, "Perhaps nothing threatens our ability to create meaning more than becoming victims of violence. In its many shapes and forms, violence interrupts the telling of the story, and our ability, as survivors, to make sense of it, rendering us helpless" (p. 153). In many countries, political movements and military coups torture and kill dissidents. As Salberg (personal communication, 2023) suggests, this violence is directed at both the *narrative* and the *storyteller*. Violence and domination *can* effectively usurp the voice of the subjugated, determining which stories get told, and which stories will never be told.

This inability to know what must be known occurs in the cultural arena *and* in intrapsychic dissociation (see Herman, 1992, 2023). In many ways, the trauma theory formulated by Laub and Auerhahn (1993) is not dissimilar to that of Davies and Frawley (1994). In their study of adult survivors of childhood sexual abuse, they note that traumatic experience "involves the foreclosure, not the elaboration of psychic contents" (p. 66). But whereas relational theories of dissociation tend to see various forms of knowledge deposited in multiple, dissociative self-states, Laub and Auerhahn seem to have had a more unitary view of the self. Laub's work seems to assert that some traumatic affects and events *have never been inscribed* in the survivor's narrative, until the humane listening of the witness facilitates that *first* inscription. This view has been over-generalized: In Grand's earlier work, descendants are assumed to be weighed down by "region after region of nullity" (Eigen, 1996, p. 106) in their parents. Salberg (2015, 2017) has theorized this through the lens of ruptured attachment and the absent states in the parental object. From this perspective, descendants are attempting to substitute the fearful "something" of memory for the dreadful "no-thing" of death (see Kierkegaard, 1937). This literature recognizes this transgenerational struggle, even as it is too definitive in its portrait:

> Those human atrocities that can be neither seen nor heard in the survivor's testimony actually retain their force through narrative absence, for this very silence opens up a terrifying imaginary space in the next generation … Through this fantasy space … the son of a survivor … creates events and experiences to fill an existential void … he attempts to place the lonely self of trauma into imaginary relation with another.
>
> (Grand, 2000, p. 24)

This perspective is reverent toward human suffering and toward the process of healing. This literature can also *fail* to witness nuanced aspects of traumatic transmission. Nonetheless, it is permeated by the ethics of Buber and Levinas, by a mandate to care for the suffering other.

Reconciling Epistemic Ambiguities

The literature cited above relies on certain assumptions about traumatic knowing that have implications for transgenerational transmission. *What* constitutes knowledge, *where knowledge* resides, in *whom*, and *how* historical knowing is formulated: These are important queries for the transgenerational project. These questions become evident when we ask: What exactly does it mean that there has been *no memorial* inscription in the survivor *until testimony meets witness*? How do we reconcile this perspective with the Relational portrait of a dissociative multiple-self-system, in which split-off self-states *are* holding/enacting/projecting history? Is there a hole in history, *or* is there a destruction of *linkages* between the self-states that carry that history?

Probably both. Is knowledge *always already* there in survivors *before* the encounter with an empathic witness? Or is knowledge birthed through the ears of a witness? These questions have great bearing on *what* needs witnessing and *what* role(s) the witness/descendant is thought to have.

These positions—that of Laub and Auerhahn (1993) and that of Relational trauma theory (see Alpert, 2001; Davies & Frawley, 1994; Grand, 2000; Howell, 1996; Reis, 2009)—seem to answer these questions differently. But these approaches are not necessarily disjunctive. The testimony in the Yale Holocaust Archive demonstrates that survivors *could* narrate their own experience. Laub and Auerhhan (1993) describe various forms of knowing history in survivors and in their descendants. For survivors, these ways of knowing range from the visceral, blank, and inchoate, through the embodied, the enacted, and the symbolic. As this trauma moves through subsequent *secure* generations, the ways of knowing can tilt more toward the symbolic. Although these forms still seem to refer to a unitary self, we can easily integrate their vicissitudes with multiple-self trauma theory (see Bromberg, 2001; Davies & Frawley, 1994; and others). In this multiple-self theory, fragmented, split-off self-states are inscribed with both *knowing* and *not-knowing*, which can take *any* or *all* of the forms described by Laub and Auerhahn.

From this perspective, traumatic history is continually in a state of emergence. History becomes named, and it recurrently appears in unsymbolized forms. Thus, when Laub (1992) argues that trauma is an event without inscription, we can deduce that, for these authors, "narrative inscription" really means a *linguistic, reflective, symbolic narrative*, which evolves from the dialogue between survivor and witness. Most clinicians working with trauma help their patient to *name* what they *already* know in other non-symbolic, embodied forms.

Thrown-ness: Culture, Ethics, and Epistemic Trouble

Ideally, the mission of witnessing is analogous to that of the liberatory struggle described by Sartre in his preface to Fanon's (1963/2004) *The Wretched of the Earth*. Referring to the liberation of Algiers from its cruel colonial masters, Sartre (1981) describes a revolt that eliminates, "in one go oppressor and oppressed: leaving one man dead and the other man free." This was the social justice critique that Fanon ignited, only to have it ignored by mainstream psychoanalysis until recently. The renewed interest in his work returns us to the social justice concerns that were part of the original project of Freud's Free Clinics. These themes pervade the work on transgenerational transmission. This work aspires to eliminate *both* oppressor and oppressed, vanquishing our destructive inner masters to liberate both ourselves *and the other*. The liberatory mission of witnessing is echoed by both Apprey (2003, 2006) and Gump (2010), who observe that descendants of African American slavery have internalized *both* master and *slave*. Similarly, Kestenberg (1982) writes, "children of (Holocaust) survivors need to rid themselves of the invasion of their superego by the double image of the persecutor and his victim" (p. 17).

At its best, this memory work allows us to feel and think beyond our own cultural embeddedness. It "moves us towards a place where we are no longer prisoners of the past but freed to relate anew to people like us and *to people not like us*" (Krondorfer, 2016, p. 93, italics added). Transgenerational studies move us closer to this capacity, but this literature is still embedded in a chain of analytic history that *critiques oppression* (see Gaztambide, 2019) even as it repeats it (see Brickman, 2017). Within our own field, *our* transgenerational legacy includes sexual boundary violations with patients, as well as biases about class, race, gender, ethnicity, and sexual orientation. Insofar as non-white, non-normative patients do enter our consulting room, they are at risk for sexism, racism, and classism. And insofar as they suffered from trauma, that trauma might be disqualified *or* assimilated into "our" white, Western assumptions.

As Krondorfer (2016) reminds us, we can recycle, "undifferentiated trauma talk (that) may lead to a false equation of all traumatized people" (p. 93). Working toward repair in post-apartheid South Africa, Gobodo-Madikizela (2016) argues that insights gained from trauma literature are not necessarily generalizable. We need to ask how a Western cultural lens is *inhibiting* our mission. Is Western psychoanalysis reifying *symbolic/linguistic narration* as a *superior* knowledge form? Might this reflect white, Western, patriarchal tropes about reason, enlightenment, and the nature of "knowledge"? Does our middle-class, Viennese construction of the family (mommy, daddy, baby) blind us to other cultural forms (see Grand, 2018b)? Do the non-white and non-Western have other registers for knowing and witnessing traumatic history? In their exploration of genocidal violence in Burundi, Lambourne and Niyonzima (2016) note that testimony and witnessing take a different shape in communal, faith-based cultures that cherish *spiritual* forms of knowing.

All of these questions circulate around the nature of traumatic knowledge and where that knowledge resides. Certainly, when we can name our trauma, we are better able to mourn it. The question here is: *How* is traumatic experience known and named in non-Western, non-white cultures? How does historical truth find its inscription? Non-dominant, subaltern cultures certainly know something about knowing trauma that white psychoanalysis has eclipsed. Gump (2017), Holmes (2006), Leary (2005), Stephens (2022), Stoute (2019, 2021), and Vaughans (2015) address the legacy of slavery and racial persecution. Black feminist analyst Foluke Taylor (2023) protests the Western, patriarchal boundaries and binaries that define and valorize linguistic, linear "knowing," arguing for the more holistic, spiritual, whole-bodied, intuitive truth forms that reflect the heritage of black women. As Menakem (2017) points out, these truths are written on the body. In recognition of this, Taylor (2023) advocates for an "unruly therapeutic" that departs from those Western forms of "knowing" that bought and sold her ancestors. In a similar vein, Stoute's (2019, 2021) work on black rage asserts that rage is a transgenerational archive of dignity, of the capacity to love in conditions of hatred. As Stoute (2021) puts this, in reference to James Baldwin:

> Baldwin refers to the "unassailable monumental dignity," of African Americans passed down in families in this transgenerational tale of trauma, decades before psychoanalysts had conceptualized resilience and dignity in psychological terms as constructs operative in protecting the self in circumstances of discrimination and dehumanizing trauma.
>
> (p. 352)

The link that Stoute is making—between black rage and the legacy of "monumental dignity"—is a powerful statement about *subaltern knowing*, about its departures from white Western psychoanalysis.

Whose trauma matters? The cultural embeddedness of Western psychoanalysis can also limit how we witness gendered violence. Working with the aftermath of the Rwandan genocide, Fox (2021) argues that, after atrocity, *gendered violence and mass rape* rarely receive memorialization and recognition. Despite the meticulous accounting of Holocaust atrocities, *mass rape* didn't appear in these histories until 2010

(Hedgepeth & Saidel, 2010); this is largely absent from transgenerational study. When a woman has been raped by the enemy, the children born of this rape are scarred by poverty, shame, social exclusion, and social hatred. As Taylor's work suggests, *mass rape* may be registered in forms of knowing and speaking that are unrecognized in patriarchal culture. We can hear this in Caroline Randall Williams' (2020) call to white supremacists in the United States, a call to witness the enslavement and rape of her ancestors: "I have rape colored skin. My light-brown-blackness is a living testament to the rules, the practices, the causes of the Old south … You want a Confederate monument? My body is a Confederate monument."

In her extensive work on sexual abuse, Judie Alpert (2017) has been decoding these knowledge forms. At her mother's deathbed, Alpert receives the secret history of her maternal forebears, and decodes her transgenerational "errand." This is a legacy of sexual violence from early 20th-century Russian pogroms; a grandmother's resiliency; emigration to America; then, the rape of Alpert's mother by her first boss. All of this was borne in silence. In this retrospective, she came to understand her own lifelong advocacy about sexual abuse. She becomes part of a larger "circle of witnessing" (Grand, 2015) that enables us to see that "hope also penetrates the darkness. Maternal care survives its own extinction" (p. 263).

Indigenous Knowledge: The Earth as Witness

By querying our own cultural embeddedness, we can speak with other cultural practices of knowing and healing. Working with Australian aboriginal healers and with the generations of aboriginal trauma caused by colonization, Tracey (2012) introduces us to the psychotherapeutic practice, "The Dreaming," and an ancient form of trauma treatment known as Dadirri. This is

> a ritualized form of "deep listening," not an ordinary witnessing but an empathic psychic action, now known to the world as psychotherapy … Aboriginal workers observe our profession of psychoanalytic therapy as symbolizing in much the same way as the Dreaming.
>
> (pp. 356–357)

These traditions, like so many others, became fractured by colonial predations. This very injury can become an unfortunate argument for the importation of psychoanalytic practices. Tracey's work is a rare exception. Joining a communal effort toward repair, she participates in the restoration of aboriginal culture and tradition. From an Aboriginal health worker, she learns that psychoanalysis "is in the same place as our dreaming" (p. 358). Tracey finds parallels between psychoanalytic concepts and Dadirri, but she removes her Western lens. She steps back. In the foreground, an elder speaks of the living, natural world that inscribes human suffering. A witnessing *landscape* is revealed through his eyes:

> The Australian continent is crisscrossed with the tracts of The Dreaming: walking, slithering, crawling, flying, chasing, hunting, dying, giving birth, performing rituals, establishing things in their own places, the landforms and water, making relationships between one place and another, changing languages, songs, changing kin.
>
> (p. 364)

Here, as in Native American cultures, the earth is Mother, a nurturing *power* that is the wellspring for all of life. If the earth is honored, it provides what we think of as the containing "maternal function." But *this* maternal function does not readily translate into our dyadic witnessing construct. Rather, this witnessing register is more like what Brave Heart et al. (2017) refer to as the "sacred path": a source of harmony, balance, spirit guides, and an attachment to all creation. It is in this spirit that Taylor (2023) dedicates her book to "the unknown grandmothers, the deep time aquifers who carry me through, who are always there when the waters break." In Western psychoanalysis, we have lost access to *this* register of knowing, recognition, and witnessing. When transgenerational trauma is inscribed on the earth, it is untranslatable in psychoanalysis. If the earth is essential to traumatic repair, we fail to grasp this. We are implicated in climate change. We privilege citified offices, individualized psyches, analytic couches, and dyadic intersubjectivity. These intimate *interpersonal* relations are deep and reparative. But as Gentile (2017) points out, they can also act "as transfer points of power not as a microcosm of power but as its marrow" (p. 177).

We need to continue this critique of the white, Western biases. As Grand (2018b) notes, these biases constrain our trauma theory and practice. At the same time, we should not over-idealize non-Western, more communal cultures. Nonetheless, this kind of decentering reminds us that witnessing, "requires risks, to be shaken in one's foundations and assumptions about the world and the Other" (Krondorfer, 2016, p. 93). This is different from a compassionate attitude, "which can be undifferentiated and can erase some objective differences" (p. 93).

Case Studies: The Ethic of Witnessing

Clara: Enslavement and the Restoration of Subjectivity

To witness our patient's suffering, to decipher her heritage, we need to locate ourselves in a social–ethical–psychosomatic nexus of listening. Janice Gump (2010) illustrates this engagement. In the case of Clara, black female patient meets black female analyst. Both carry the legacy of enslavement: domination and subjugation, the near extinction of black subjectivity in African American slavery. From the first session, knowledge speaks through Clara's body:

> a slim attractive woman of 27 years, her acute pain and anxiety were riveting. The tension of her body and the shrillness of her voice bespoke colossal efforts to suppress these affects. She had been taught she had "nothing to cry about."
>
> (p. 49)

Nothing to cry about. Although they are raised in very different familial constellations, Gump (2017), too, knows this edict. She, herself, has received it; she knows that parental voice which signals despair: *You are a slave, no one will care if you cry out*. But Gump is deeply empathic, she *wants* to be *with* Clara, so that Clara can know that this "nothing" is a vast "something." This something is her own and her ancestors' tears. But Clara cannot be *with* another black woman in either joy or suffering. Clara's father treated Clara and her mother with contempt. Centuries of oppression were represented through a mirroring of erasure:

> She seemed aware of me only as an object to whom she must reluctantly transmit feelings, not as someone with whom she might be in relationship. Not until termination, when we met briefly and did some long-distance work, did I have a sense of mutual engagement, of some vibrant space between us.
>
> (2010, p. 49)

Gump discovers that, in Clara's childhood, she felt imprisoned by a father who was domineering, raging, and needy. The father demanded continuous, exacting deference and attention. In this dynamism, Clara is a subordinated object in a series of subordinated female objects: "the wife's subjectivity was demeaned ... The patient describes efforts to subjugate any notion of self" (p. 50).

After two years of therapy, Clara seizes her voice and rebels against her father. Then, Gump makes historical links to slavery and to the subjectivity-effacing conditions of violence and mass rape:

> ... the father's mother, whom he behaviorally resembled, was widely disliked in their community for her meanness and lying. Furthermore, her father—the father's grandfather—had also been cruel. He managed the former slave dwellings on the plantation where they still lived. I think it not too speculative to imagine that someone in his family had held the kind (and quality) of authority given not only to overseers but also to some slaves.
>
> (p. 50)

Gump traces slavery's domination through three generations. Through their shared erasure as black female subjects, and in the restitution of Clara's voice, subjugated objects are recognized and become liberated subjects. Clara has been witnessed, and in that witnessing, her ancestors are registered in history. This is profound clinical work. Throughout psychoanalysis, we need to collectively register and witness this history.

Dietrich L.: Inhumanity and the Restoration of Guilt

For the analyst, witnessing is not always an experience of empathic receptivity. When a patient arrives in treatment bearing a legacy of atrocity, the analyst can encounter violent motifs, megalomania, and a complete absence of guilt. Countertransferential alienation and horror can become the venue for witnessing. Eckstaedt (1982), a German analyst, elucidates this in the treatment of Deitrich L. Analyst and patient met years after World War II ended. However, they were each marked by that war and engaged across a vast ethical divide. Eckstaedt was 4 when the war broke out; her parents neither belonged to, nor sympathized with, the Nazi party. Dietrich is the son of avowed Nazis. During the war, Dietrich's family extols the father as a heroic Nazi soldier, an idealized Aryan "God" fighting at the front. Also working as a judge in court-martial proceedings, the father had the authority to kill: He sentenced men to execution. Then, he was a prisoner of war, a failed hero in a lost war, a contemptible object to Dietrich's Nazi mother. For this mother, the war never ends: Dietrich is trained to be another hard, remorseless Aryan soldier. His family is wealthy and privileged. They feel superior; they are sufficient unto themselves and without human *need*. This is a delusional world in which there is no human Other and the limits of reality do not exist. His childhood cruelties; his recurrent failures in school: Everything was denied, excused, and paid off.

In the first session, Dietrich held up his hands and said to the analyst, "These are my hands, they are the hands of my father. My father has blood on his hands." He goes on, itemizing his father's killings. The analyst is shocked and confused, unable to respond to this declaration, but hoping/wishing that the patient is communicating guilt of having "blood on his hands." The analyst never forgets this scene; the patient will have no memory of it. Later, the analyst recognizes this initial statement as a threat,

> My reaction to his opening words—the fact that I had avoided confronting the patient by not putting into words the emotional experience—was to determine the whole constellation of transference in his analysis. Without meaning to, I had become passively involved in a situation in which I actively witnessed his potential violence. The patient experienced this as an initial victory …
>
> (p. 200)

It becomes evident that conflict with Dietrich, or any conflict with the father, "could end in only one way: it would cost someone his life" (p. 201).

Thus begins a long treatment narrative, in which the analyst endures her patient's impenetrability, concreteness, and simulated humanity. The patient has been borrowing the analyst's identity and eventually starts a psychotherapeutic practice of his own, despite a lack of both training and human compassion. This is a mimicry of the analyst, a grandiose identification, a denial of dependency on the analyst. But, more than anything, this is an *injustice*, an exploitation of vulnerable patients. The ethical horror that Eckstaedt has been feeling throughout the treatment builds, until she issues an ultimatum. Dietrich will have to choose between his analysis or continuing his practice. This is a potent *no* spoken to Dietrich *on behalf of the suffering Other*. Dietrich chooses treatment; his psychic carapace breaks down and disintegrates. In a psychotic episode, Dietrich relives the terrors—not the heroics—of his father's war. As he recovers, reflectivity emerges. Cruelty is no longer idealized, and affect is no longer repressed. Dependency is recognized, and the other has begun to exist. Dietrich is not transformed. But ethical horror in the analytic witness has birthed a capacity for guilt.

Summary

Witnessing has now been incorporated into the vernacular of mainstream psychoanalysis. We appreciate, as Buber (1923) would put it, that, witnessing is a "great relation ... [which] throws a bridge from self-being to self-being across the abyss of dread of the universe" (p. 175). Buber's description echoes the ethos of the relational turn in psychoanalysis. The integration of social justice with object relations and interpersonal theory has ushered in a social-ethical turn in psychoanalysis as well (see Layton & Goodman, 2014). With this recognition, clinical witnessing becomes infused with Herman's (1992) ethic of justice: "Moral neutrality in the conflict between victim and perpetrator is not an option. Like all other bystanders, therapists are sometimes forced to take sides" (p. 247).

4

When Wounds Touch
Witnessing and Enacting as Embodied Healing Processes

Jill Salberg

> There is, in each survivor, an imperative need to *tell* and thus to
> come to *know* one's story, unimpeded by ghosts from the past
> against which one has to protect oneself. One has to know one's
> buried truth in order to be able to live one's life.
>
> (Laub, 1995, p. 63)

I start with questions, queries in my own mind. How did witnessing
become part of psychoanalysis? How did this concept migrate from
another discipline into psychoanalysis, and is it psychoanalytic? Psychoanalysis has a history of migrating concepts from other disciplines,
utilizing them as a lens to then re-view theories or even to disrupt prevailing ideas. Deconstruction from the postmodern movement in the
philosophy of Derrida (1967) and bringing the feminist critique into
psychoanalysis (de Beauvoir, 1949; Irigaray, 1977; Mitchell, 1973,
and others) are examples of theory migrations.

In this chapter, I will be examining the ways that psychoanalysis
has imported an originally legal register and written it into psychoanalysis. Thus, it is valuable to wonder if witnessing can be considered
a psychoanalytic process, and if so, how we actually understand its
meaning. Further, in what way is there therapeutic action or traction
within treatment beyond a testimonial process? Can we think of witnessing as an intrinsic part of a healing psychoanalytic process specific
to big trauma, or can witnessing be considered part of the therapeutic
work in general, not unique to trauma work?

Additionally, I will be looking at how witnessing as a psychoanalytic
concept and tool is utilized and sometimes lost and re-found during treatment—a potentially powerful mutative process. I start with the question: How has psychoanalysis incorporated witnessing as a conceptual

DOI: 10.4324/9781003087762-8

framework? In the prior chapter, we have noted that witnessing, prior to its use in Holocaust testimonial projects, was most extensively used as a legal term and one that includes the giving of testimony. Merriam-Webster states that a witness is one who attests to a fact or event, gives evidence or testifies in a court, or has personal knowledge of something. A witness is a person who saw or heard a crime take place or may have important information about the crime or the defendant. There is a very specific role that a witness plays in a court of law in that both the defense and prosecutor can call witnesses to testify. This is a role that has the power to substantiate and/or determine facts and events. The testimony of a witness is held as valid unless refuted by other testimonies. And in the realm of faith-based religions, there is the bearing witness to one's religious convictions, and to the revelation of a divine being's existence.

Although Freud, at times, emphasized reconstruction and the pursuit of historical truth, psychoanalysis has not been focused on "facts" and "evidence" as a means of knowing the patient. Indeed, the historical truth of childhood trauma quickly yielded to a focus on oedipal fantasy (as discussed in Chapter 1). In the late 20th century, after the genocidal epoch of World War II, Spezzano (1993) and Spence (1982) would argue that psychoanalysis had no access to historical truth; it could only co-construct a narrative truth. As Grand (2000) noted, this view was inadequate in its address to trauma. It is significant that, around the same time, Holocaust studies embraced the language of the legal register: the language of testimony and witnessing. These terms have clearly provided an expansive way for psychoanalysis to think about trauma and traumatic experiences. This shift has allowed us to formulate the effects of trauma on the minds of survivors and their succeeding generations. New ways of working with trauma have emerged.

As we have been exploring in the previous chapter, it is crucial in our lives and our therapeutic work to fully be able to witness the other's experiences, to hold their suffering even when it stirs up powerful responses in us. Witnessing is a dialogic process in analytic work, always engaging both parties. The patient is longing to be heard, seen, recognized (Benjamin, 2018), to find a willing participant to contain their story and ghosts. While the analyst is the receiving partner, we can't always know what we will be asked to contain or how it will register inside of us. The goal is for a holding environment (Slochower, 2004) that can contain and allow someone to come out of dissociation and heal from what they have had to survive.

This is not an intersubjective space that is easily attained but one that is constantly being worked upon. Multi-generational trauma transmissions are not always coded simply in language. They are found in bodily experiences, fragments, recurring as parts of dreams, and projected into other people. Becoming a witness in these treatments involves being affected in known and unknown ways. We understand very little as it is unfolding, putting our trust in our process, something which we cannot fully control. It is powerful, and we often alternate with our patients between who is helpless and who is being helpful.

Witnessing and Testimony

Testimony becomes the fulcrum in which a victim can begin to witness the trauma they have had to endure. The person receiving the testimony is the necessary *Other* as Laub (1992) states, "the hearer, who is, so to speak, the blank screen on which the event comes to be inscribed for the first time" (p. 57). To my ears, Laub is describing an exceedingly relational/interpersonal event. In beginning to hear about the trauma, we, as receptive listeners, help the person speaking to begin to apprehend what they have suffered. Additionally, the listener potentially begins to vicariously experience some of the affective experiences endured by the trauma survivor—a dangerous enterprise for all involved, I might add. We the "trauma listeners" run a dual risk: We fear that in the telling our patients we will inevitably *re-live* and—as a consequence in the remembering—may be re-traumatized, while we, the listener, or as Gerson (2009) termed a "live witness," also chance being traumatized in the listening.

In Bion's terms, we are the container, metabolizing the contents deposited within us (the contained) and giving this version back to the other. Bion's emendation to Klein's concept of projective and introjected aspects of the mother–baby dyad adds an active relational dimension. Two minds are engaged to make sense of one mind, a bi-personal field. When this process happens between the therapy dyad, make no mistake, trauma can be disturbingly contagious. We often feel some disturbing version of what the patient has endured. However, Boulanger (2018) has persuasively argued that it may be a *necessary therapeutic tool*:

> Vicarious trauma must become a dynamic intersubjective process. Sometimes vicarious trauma is experienced as a form of psychic contagion, unwelcome and unintentional. Only in acknowledging

the contagion can clinicians begin to work through their patients' traumatic experiences. In helping patients metabolize what had initially proved psychically indigestible, clinicians also have to work through their own experience of the patient's experience.

(p. 67)

I want to consider what Laub sets forth, the first inscription of the trauma experience, as one that can come through as narrative and possibly *also* as enactment. When we work with people who have endured hardships and trauma in their lives, there are often unprocessed, unmetabolized, and unformulated aspects of their experiences that enter the work in unplanned for ways (e.g., Bromberg, 2003; Grand, 2000, 2009; D. B. Stern, 2010).

Entanglement or "enactments" (see Aron, 2003; Bass, 2003; Katz, 1998; and others) are revelatory of unsymbolized knowledge in our clinical work. Given that psychoanalysis is a meeting between the patient's unconscious and the analyst's, it is likely that our own internal self-states have been activated/enacted in response to this form of testimony (see Benjamin, 2018; Bromberg, 2003; Davoine & Gaudillère, 2004; Gampel, 2019; Grand, 2000, 2009; Reis, 2009; Ullman, 2006). This encounter can become a toxic impasse, but as Davoine and Gaudillère suggest (2004), history can become newly visible for both analyst and patient. From this perspective, traumatic history is *continually* emerging in intersubjective contexts. This emergent history continually moves from the inchoate to the symbolic.

The trauma literature has been utilizing concepts such as witnessing, testimony, and reconciliation as important processes toward post-traumatic conflict resolution, healing, and repair. I believe that these conceptions dovetail well with each other. In her discussion of "circles of witnessing," Grand (2015) writes about the profound loneliness that trauma survivors experience and the search for reparative attachment. This tension of absence and presence, of mental collapse and holding recognition, is what witnessing offers working toward a psychoanalytic reparative healing process. Grand further believes that, in her words, "circles of witnessing" are necessary to re-instate I–Thou capacities, that in the traumatic attempt at annihilation, at the destruction of maternal care functioning, "hope also penetrates the darkness. Maternal care survives its own extinction" (p. 263). Witnessing is a crucial first step in the repairing of ruptures in attachment experiences, often implicated in trauma.

Case Example: Vicarious Trauma in the Analytic Space

It is not always easy to distinguish vicarious trauma stirred by the patient and multi-generational histories that correspond or even collide. Each of us brings our own multi-generational lives internally dormant but present nonetheless. In Guralnik's (2014) haunting paper "The Dead Baby," she looks at the ghosts and unspeakable violence that filled her patient Nyx's history (German with Nazi grandparents) and her own (Israeli parents with family lost in the Holocaust). Her patient is filled with guilt, reenacting gruesome patterns of gross negligence (binge drinking a few times while pregnant) with unrelenting self-punishment (imagined plans to violently kill herself and her baby). The fragments of Big History as lived by the patient's family tumble into the sessions, with stories of dead babies: Nyx's mother's loss of two babies as well as emotional abandonment of Nyx, along with her father's sadistic rages. These portraits of Nazi hardness and violence permeate the treatment and Guralnik's mind as she imagines pregnant mothers and children gassed by the Nazis along with Israeli violence directed in Gaza toward mothers and children there. The amount of (in Bion's vernacular) beta contents that Guralnik was asked to hold at times was excessive. The analytic function was stretched, taxed, and re-found, allowing the dyad to continue the work of witnessing and of sorting whose trauma belonged to whom. Big History was revealed, and the personal history was slowly recalled in all of its violence and ugliness.

Guralnik demonstrates this by continually searching for the vulnerable places in her patient, that she was once the victim of monstrous parents who themselves suffered from the evil infecting their parent's lives. These parents were the second generation, born to Nazi parents who perpetrated unspeakable crimes and whose country lost the war, had to rebuild, and for years refused to confront the evil atrocity and lost their moral compass. Who is the criminal, and what is the crime? Dead babies suggest murderous mothers. Guralnik notices her own dissociation, her inability to sit with murderousness. Her coming out of dissociating means becoming the witness to Nyx's story, her family's history, and to the crimes of an entire generation. The analytic process is one of struggling to witness, failing to, and then continually finding new footing to remember the patient's place of injury within her destructive lostness.

Analytic Theories of Witnessing

As I explore psychoanalytic theories of witnessing, I must acknowledge that our theories are formulated within our Western, largely white psychoanalysis. I will touch on a few of these theories, although there are many more than we can cover in this space (e.g., Boulanger, 2018; Kogan, 1995). Writing about witnessing as an analytic process, Poland (2000) makes a distinction between the analytic functions of interpreting and witnessing, seeing both as complementary roles for the analyst. He believes that even with great empathy and sympathy, the analyst still stands outside the traumatic event a patient has lived or is going through. Nonetheless, the stance of witness is crucial, as Poland, quoting Felman and Laub (1992) who paraphrased Freud, believed, "it takes two to witness the unconscious" (p. 15). The position of where we stand is what Poland explicates so well. As he puts it, our "otherness" allows us to hear, see, and comprehend with great recognition and yet not act. He writes, "By *witnessing* I refer to an analyst's activity, that of 'getting' what the patient is saying without doing anything more active about it, not even gathering 'grist for the mill'" (p. 21). Ullman (2006) concurs with this, drawing upon Poland's work and the philosophy of Levinas, when she affirms that otherness is an essential role for the analyst: "Witnessing is thus a somewhat different way of listening in which otherness is not only recognized but in fact required for the release of the story" (pp. 190–191).

Boulanger (2008, 2018) has highlighted the devastating effects of what she has termed adult-onset trauma. In distinguishing from early relational trauma, Boulanger has responded to a gap in our literature that looks at surviving natural disasters (and with climate change, there are more and more of these), violent aggressive acts such as lynchings, terrorism/terrorist assaults, crashes, catastrophes such as wars, 9/11, ethnic cleansing, and more. In her work with Vietnam veterans and asylum seekers, Boulanger (2008) has found that "Adult survivors of massive psychic trauma find every aspect of their waking and dreaming lives, every self-state, permeated by the sense of a collapsed self" (p. 643).

This collapse of the core self can be seen in what Boulanger terms *catastrophic dissociation*, resulting in profound numbing affectively and physically, psyche and soma. This state includes losing one's subjectivity, becoming an object with one's own will robbed, without any sense of one's own agency. Boulanger argues for maintaining, when possible, a clear distinction between witnessing and recognition, not conflating them. Witnessing horrific trauma necessarily needs a containing function, including one's capacity to join the patient in their reliving of trauma. Boulanger in writing about her patient Celeste:

> As she described her imprisonment and rape, the tension between joining and observing—the tightrope that clinicians walk in every session—dissolved, I became one with Celeste. My own boundaries were temporarily suspended as I absorbed horror, disgust, humiliation, pain, and grief that were to haunt me for several weeks. In my subsequent conversations with Celeste, I learned that knowing that I was a separate person who had voluntarily stepped into her experience, that I was prepared to bear witness to this experience, and bear up under the experience began the process of reanimating her object world, and reduced her sense of having been rendered untouchable by her rapists.
>
> (p. 652)

In joining her patient, Boulanger eases the abjection and loneliness the trauma victim has been enduring. This is Boulanger's ethic of care, freely given to her patient as joining and recognition, allowing the patient to begin to return to her own body and self as subject, worthy of love and compassion.

Gerson (2009) has written regarding what allows for this kind of care, for a witness to become engaged, to care while listening, remain engaged while imagining the horrors of the trauma while helping the person to integrate what has been unknowable. Gerson's deeply thoughtful and prescient work opens with this paradoxical observation:

> The imperatives to bear witness and the seductions of blind denial are competing and everlasting legacies of the Holocaust. Each challenges our frailties in the face of an indifferent world and marks the potential, as well as the limits, of being human ... What then can exist between the scream and the silence? We hope first that there is an engaged witness—an other that stands beside the event and the self and who cares to listen; an other who is able to contain that which is heard and is capable of imagining the unbearable; an other who is in a position to confirm both our external and our psychic realities and, thereby, to help us integrate and live within all realms of our experience. This is the presence that lives in the gap, absorbs

absence, and transforms our relation to loss. It is the active and attuned affective responsiveness of the witnessing other that constitutes a "live third"—the presence that exists between the experience and its meaning, between the real and the symbolic, and through whom life gestates and into whom futures are born.

(pp. 1341–1342)

Utilizing the literature on intersubjectivity and thirdness (e.g., Aron, 2006; Benjamin, 2004, 2018; Ogden, 1994), Gerson explicates this capacity for witnessing as a *live third*. The opposite of this happens when there is trauma that no one can or will witness. Gerson refers to this as the *dead third*:

I believe that the enduring presence of absence within the psyche may best be conceived of as a *dead third*, and, when we live in relation to it, we live within the trace, memory, reverberation, and echo of loss. The losses embodied in this ephemeral but ever-present *dead third* exist as the impossibilities that confront the life of desire and hope.

(p. 1349)

How, then, does one counter deadness? Gerson speaks of a "presence that lives in the gap, absorbs absence, and transforms our relation to loss" (p. 1342). I imagine Gerson is suggesting a *therapeutic attuneness* that allows one to not dissociate out of terror of loss and trauma but to move into a place of heightened empathic awareness. This is an internal space of residing close to, yet separate enough from, the patient to be able to bear witness and recognize their experience. It requires a recognition of both similarity (I have felt as my patient does) and difference (this is uniquely my patient's experience) and the capacity to transcend that gap.

A somewhat different angle on witnessing has been taken by Reis (2009). He argues, following Loewald, that Freud's separating remembering from repeating, as if they were different forms of memory, is not consistent with what we now understand about how memories are encoded:

I would further suggest that enactive memory phenomena in their bodily registration represent the essential force of traumatic occurrence contained in a form of memory that may only be experienced

as event, rather than narration ... [these] experiences, held in epi-
sodic memory systems have no translation into language, but which
convey the patients' modes of reaction *as memory*.

(p. 1362)

For Reis, we need to live with and witness these events along with our
patients without desire to transform them into language or to make
meaning. They are meaningful as lived and enacted events with us in
the room. Hence, enactment and witnessing are no longer dichotomous.
Rather, they become a communicative and shared relational experience, authentically lived within the transference–countertransference
matrix. Reis' view is in agreement with Benjamin (1988):

> The point at which the patient presents the real difficulty that needs
> mending, really is often experienced as the moment of maximum
> attack on our subjectivity (as analysts and as persons). This de-
> struction is inevitable when we work in "basic fault" areas, where
> traumatic repetition is so emotionally powerful that understanding
> appears to the patient as useless.
>
> (p. 203)

Before moving on, we want to note another aspect of Reis' perspective.
While most of the authors we have cited speak to the traumatic loss of
the (real/inner) maternal function, likening witnessing to the mother's
recognizing gaze and holding function, Reis (2015) draws our attention to the paternal function typically associated with symbolic language and culture: "It behooves us to think about the testimonies of
Holocaust survivors [and other traumas, our addition] as also reflecting
the breakdown of a paternal order—of language, culture, and *the ability to make meaning*" (p. 342).

Whereas Reis' emphasis is largely embodied, enacted, and intersubjective, D. B. Stern (2012, 2022) joins the intersubjective with the
intrapsychic. Stern agrees that there is a two-person relational/inter-
personal witnessing experience occurring in treatment. But in addition
to this, he feels that there may also be the development of an "internal
witness":

> [This] witness may be internal and, in that sense, imaginary. Some-
> one else, even if that someone is another part of ourselves, must
> know what we have gone through, must be able to feel it *with* us.

We must be *recognized* by an other (Benjamin, 1988, 1995, 1998) even if that other is now part of us.

(pp. 58–59)

Here, the emphasis is on the restoration of the internal "protective parental shield," similar to Laub's concept of the internalized maternal imago that trauma destroys (see Chapter 1). For Stern, that internal object has *never* been destroyed. Thus, witnessing is another way of forming internal objects and expanding the internal world of the patient.

Amir (2012) moves us further into the intrapsychic realm. She draws upon Winnicott's contributions on holding, the development from absolute dependence to independence, and the effects of gross impingement (Winnicott's notion of trauma):

The psychic function of the inner witness is a mechanism that develops in response to a reasonable experience of infantile helplessness, the resulting maternal impingement and the presence of a sufficient experience of a third (whether concrete or imaginary) who is internalized as an inner observer. The function of the inner witness is crucial to the subject's capacity to shift between the first person and the third person of experience, or between the "experiencing I" and the "reflective I," and its absence leads to a sense of hollowness, emptiness and futility.

(p. 879)

Amir is conceptualizing a profoundly intrapsychic psychoanalytic approach to witnessing; she sees this as a developmental process and psychic function. The development of an inner witness, in Amir's terms, is a psychic achievement born of both sufficient maternal attunement and sufficient maternal impingement. Amir is suggesting a radical understanding of Winnicott: that a child is at times a victim of the mother's hatred or violence, that this causes the experience of helplessness. "Thus, the inner witness develops as a reaction to a reasonable experience of helplessness and in the face of a sufficient experience of 'being seen' by a third" (p. 884). Amir has outlined modes of internal witnessing, taking into account the ability to access and make use of both a first-person and third-person (reflective) point of view. This is all seen as normative development with greater and lesser degrees of development in each person.

Important to underscore is that Amir does not see this as a response to trauma. However, she understands that in situations of trauma, previously developed capacities are tasked with managing extreme experiences. For Amir, only those who have *already* developed an inner witness would be capable of transforming unbearable experiences of deadness into living, mentalizable contents and affects. It is this transformation that turns memory into narrative. This point of view is consistent with Ornstein's (2003) work, who has argued that pathologizing survivors of trauma (specifically the Holocaust) is grossly wrong. There is a life lived prior to any trauma, and Amir's work delineates what is developmentally achieved while also vulnerable under extreme experiences, which then can result in an internal state of self-annihilation.

Witnessing as a Profoundly Relational Event

I return to my opening question: Can witnessing, now incorporated into the vernacular of psychoanalysis, be considered a psychoanalytic term and process? The *relational turn* in psychoanalysis ushered in a movement toward authenticity and emotional truth as equally important as the correct interpretation or historical reconstruction (see Aron, 2006; Benjamin, 2004, 2009; Bucci, 2007; and others). The analyst's affective attunement, willingness to be emotionally impacted by the patient, and engage using their vulnerability to reach the patient allowed for a broader use of countertransference. Furthermore, we have begun to understand how our present is layered with the terrors of generations past; the terrors of the present will be layered onto succeeding generations (see Grand & Salberg, 2015; Salberg & Grand, 2017). Our growing literature on the intergenerational transmission of trauma shows us that the wounds of others must be investigated to make meaning of our own, that what happened to forebearers becomes transmitted and lives within us.

It is my belief that when "wounds touch"—that is, when a patient's wound stirs our own—a profoundly deep form of witnessing can occur. Our wound is not identical to the patient's, but it is in some affective relationship with what the patient is struggling to feel, remember, or disavow. Once stirred, we become enlisted in reliving some painful experience that until this moment in treatment was not fully known. It might have been told as a story, or in Meares' (1998) language as a Script, a concrete retelling without agency, reflectivity, or even affect. It is not spoken by an agentic fully embodied self and therefore can remain a fragment, dissociated from other fragments or memories that continue to haunt from within. Often, trauma appears in communications that are both urgent and ambiguous:

> Vaguely alarming yet unreal, laden with consequence yet evaporating before the mind ... pain comes unsharably into our midst as at once that which cannot be denied and that which cannot be confirmed ... to have great pain is to have certainty; to hear that another person has pain is to experience doubt.
>
> (Scarry, 1985, pp. 4–7)

Psychoanalytic treatment is in many ways a healing process, despite any claim or proof to "cure." We offer a safe enough place for the survivors of trauma and their descendants to begin to unravel the ways in which the truth of their lives has been carried and yet remains unknowable. As the receiver of these truths, our empathic stance has to be one of willingness to surrender and enter dark and painful places, to use our own wounds as our unconscious *sonar* system, as if locating something underwater. Mucci (2022) argues,

> To go through the perilous journey of testimony, the survivor needs the body and the mind and the care of another, trained to do this with the appropriate attention and attunement ... This kind of empathic surrendering cannot be taught, though it can be the fruit of several life experiences.
>
> (p. 155)

Mucci terms this work as "embodied witnessing," which I feel captures the fullness and experience near quality of this healing process.

This is a fuller elaboration of Ferenczi's (1932/1995, 1933/1949) work describing how the analyst works empathically, linking emotions with actions and believing the patient's story, perhaps for the first time. Further, Mucci argues that this form of work, in line with Aron (1996), Schore (2001, 2003a, 2003b), and others, involves right-brain to right-brain connection and activity, a kind of access to implicit memory and the formation of a new relational holding in order that, in her words, "embodied witnessing" can occur.

Psychoanalytic witnessing is hard work because it draws upon our full selves, soma and psyche. It is my belief that when a patient's deep—sometimes without words—experience touches our own wounds that are similar enough to be stirred, a powerful experience does occur within the dyad. This becomes a moment of connection that is felt on a procedural level. As discussed in the attachment literature, safety and fear are the earliest aspects of the attachment relationship. Our patient's fears of remembering great pain become possible as we are stirred to remember our own and reach toward our patients with a lifeline. In Guralnik's (2014) paper, we can see this toward the end when, in a stirring moment with her patient Nyx, Guralnik says: "She was weeping again: '*I can't think anymore.*' '*Let's try to think together.*' Nyx was grieving. 'Say something,' she pleaded. It was simple: '… I had this image of me holding your hand'" (p. 143).

Utilizing two clinical cases, one from my practice and the second from Grand's, I hope to illuminate what this embodied psychoanalytic witnessing can look like. The first case is in the early part of a treatment with my patient, reflecting how a fully relational and embodied witnessing occurs early in the work. These early stirrings enable the psychoanalytic work to deepen. The second case shows how a profoundly experiential form of witnessing unlocks trauma affects that were sequestered, dissociative, and until this time controlling the patient and her life.

Clinical Case 1: Kim: Embodied Shame and Grief, Restoration of Memory

Kim is an Asian-American cisgender female in her mid-50s, unattached for a very long time. She has come into treatment due to stress and anxiety related to her high-powered corporate job. Her romantic life is non-existent, and I often wondered during our sessions, "Where do Kim's feelings about her personal private life escape to when she is consumed with her grievances about her work?" Each work-related slight or injustice widens the anger stream. Her strongest connections are still with her parents, and as an Asian-American eldest child, she is dutiful. Her love of travel, her wanderlust is unabated, but she travels mostly with her parents, sometimes just her mother. Who will she have once her parents are gone?

I remember back to earlier feelings Kim had about her parents, ones that crept into the work through the back door, through my body. Kim was having trouble talking about something having to do with her father. The more she struggled, the more I felt this unwanted sense of shame enter my body; I would find my eyes cast more downward and a slight discomfort I recognized when feeling ashamed of something. I almost felt like squirming in my chair. A memory floated into awareness, one I hadn't thought of for a very long time. The sense of shame, no longer a refugee, was sitting more fully in my chest. I gave it voice:

> I am not sure why but while listening to you a memory from my childhood has come back to me. When I was only about 6 or 7 years old my parents wanted to take me and my older sister to see Niagara Falls. It was a 2-day drive and that first night we had trouble finding a motel to stay over in. I hadn't known this at the time but later learned that every time my father went into a place to ask for rooms for the night, when he told them our last name, a Jewish-sounding name, he was told there were no vacancies. We didn't find a place till 11:00 PM. I have such a sense of the shame my father had to endure.

Tears came into my eyes and voice as I told her this story. I was aware of feeling quite vulnerable sharing this personal information with my patient.

Kim immediately said that during the years that she and her family lived abroad while growing up, each year they were required to come back to the US to renew their visas. Upon landing at JFK and at Passport Control, they stood waiting, and when her father tried to approach the man checking passports with theirs, the passport agent barked a racial slur, "C---, stand over there." Kim is crying and says, "My father, who is so accomplished, who I respect so much was spoken to so ..." and her voice drifts off into tears. We cry for our fathers who were shamed, refugee and escapee feelings now linking us in a way we hadn't known each other before.

Clinical Case 2: Rosa: Disembodiment and Resurrecting the Dead

In Grand's (2000, 2009) work with Rosa, a disembodied countertransference becomes a conduit for the dead and the missing. Rosa was sexually abused in childhood by a great-uncle.

> She has always felt female. Insofar as she is female, she hates her body. Insofar as she is without self-hatred, her body has vanished. In these disembodied states, she was insensate; she felt she had no

genitalia or any gender marker. She needed to heal herself, and to do that, she needed to *know*. In Rosa's family, there were Catholic immigrants from Italy and Russian Jewish immigrants. Familial stories were fraught with secrets, gaps, and contradictions. Rosa's mother was both invasive and detached; Rosa was unsure if this "mother" was really her mother. There were relatives missing in Turin who were subsequently restored. There were relatives missing who were never restored … There was a biological family where relations were ill-defined. There were brothers who were not real brothers and real sisters who were unknown to each other until their own adulthood. There were no grandparents left alive, but there was a great-uncle who seems to have been her mother's actual father. With regard to these figures, there were false explanations and no explanations and stories that cracked under the slightest scrutiny. And there was a seamless disregard for contradiction: They were long dead, and they were not dead.

(p. 141)

Rosa needs to *know* when and where these women went missing: who is alive and who is dead. All of this seems linked to her silent great-uncle, who molested her when she was "sleeping."

Rosa never told her parents about the sexual violation. When asked why, she replied that she pitied him for a loneliness that never found its name.

The first phase of Rosa's treatment was an embodied processing of the sexual abuse; she finally told her parents and felt their concern. Gradually, she felt more whole and decided to relocate to Europe for a job traveling in the fashion industry. A year later, she calls Grand from Europe in a state of terror. This begins a disembodied phase of treatment, in which her world seems like an unreal simulation of the human. Now working on the telephone, without Rosa's embodied presence, Grand's psyche-soma is overtaken by parallel phantasms. In these phantasms, there is a mechanized landscape populated by "humanoids," by the mutant and the dead. These images mirror Rosa's terror, and Rosa feels witnessed in this echo of her disembodiment: This encodes another time, in which female civilians became an "it," raped and murdered, during World War II. In Rosa's family, her vagina was simultaneously violated and erased. As she returns to life, she feels accompanied by all the missing women: They are alive, with Rosa, on Brooklyn streets.

The truth that Grand learns—that the great-uncle sexually molested Rosa in the dark at a movie theater in a robotic, without human emotion manner—was something known and spoken about earlier in the treatment. We could say it was a testimony that had been given but not witnessed. Here in this fully embodied way, Grand becomes the true witness to the experience of Rosa's degradation and loss of humanness. These are the origins of Rosa's self-hatred and body loathing, but words could not carry the depth of the violation, the severity of the attack on the self. It is in the analytic dyad's capacity to enter the domain of violence, evil, and deadness that true psychoanalytic witnessing occurs. It is here that healing can begin to occur, not a superficial creation of narrative, but an embodied feeling of recognition and of not being alone in the hour of destruction.

In Conclusion

I have tried to show in this chapter the complexity and ways in which psychoanalysis has imported witnessing and testimony from other disciplines and created its own unique conceptualization. Psychoanalytic witnessing is always a two-person event, mutually engaged with despite the dyad's asymmetry (Aron, 1996). The analytic relationship works hard to restore trust in attachments and repair the non-recognition inherent in the violence of trauma. Psychoanalytic witnessing works to restore humanity where it was crushed, enabling the patient to inhabit their subjectivity and claim for human recognition and worth. Ultimately, this will enable agency to flourish in rebuilding lives.

Legacies from Trauma of Immigration, Violence, Loss, and Shame

"I am living, I remember you."

Rossanna Echegoyén, LCSW: Personal Story*

I see you looking back at me in the mirror every morning,
I search my face for your face,
¡Papa!
I cry when I cannot find you,
I sob in despair that you could not be saved,
I look in the mirror, every morning and every night,
I see your face in my face,
When I do not see you,
I search my face for your face,
When I see you, I get lost in the memory of you,
Sometimes, I do not think I am living my life because I'm waiting to hear your voice,
"¡Aquí está Luis Echegoyén!"
I am living, I remember you,
I have not forgotten you,
To live my life and move forward,
I must let you go.
Yet, I continue to see your face in my face when I look in the mirror.
¡Papa!
Quisiera escuchar tu voz una vez mas,
I just need to hear your voice once more,
I go back to the mirror to look for your face,
A sign, a grimace, a smile, a light.
I cannot find you!
Later in the day, I find your handwritten notes in my books,

DOI: 10.4324/9781003087762-9

And I get lost in your writing,
¡Papa!

I'm drenched with memories of you,
Soaked with sadness and tears,
Yet blessed that you were my father,
Papa,
I am living,
I am living, I remember you,
I will always remember you.

My first recollection of trauma was at age 7 years old when my father came home bloodied with gashes on his face and eyebrow, busted lip, bruises and a black eye. I was frightened by the sight of him as he stumbled into my mother's arms. His shirt was soaked with his own blood. My mother exclaimed, "What happened to you?!" He was beaten by two cops on his way home after a night of drinking. "Go back to your country you filthy Mexican." My father was not Mexican, he was from El Salvador.

My grandfather died suddenly when my father was 3 years old. My father told us that he was murdered. But my relatives affirm that my grandfather took his own life.

My father immigrated to the US where he became a household name on Spanish-speaking TV. While successful, his inner demons of trauma, loss, and shame were woven into his psyche.

Before he retired, my father visited his father's grave and his drinking led to an impenetrable, severe depression. Elements of shame and loss emerged in our family dynamics which revolved around my father. He was the center of our family orbit until he died. The repetition of a traumatic death perpetuates the traumatic shame and family secrets. The ghosts of our past continue to haunt us. He is no longer living, yet I see his face in my face every day. And now, I'm looking for the ghost of my past in the mirror.

Note

* Rossanna Echegoyén is affiliated with Manhattan Institute for Psychoanalysis in New York City and is author of "Abandoning the Analytic Frame," published in Division 39's *Div/Review* special issue on community psychoanalysis.

5

Legacies of Violence
Our Perpetrator Fragments

Sue Grand

> There always lurked an existential angst that the destructive tumor, the cruel perpetrator within ourselves, might develop against our will, and erupt like a volcano.
>
> (Enola Sielbert, child of a Nazi SS officer, in Hammerich et al., 2016, p. 256)

The repair of the persecuted (and their descendants) is the preeminent focus of this book. However, fuller repair of our patients requires attention to the internalized perpetrator fragments that can take up residence in the persecuted and in their descendants. This view has been emphasized by Grand (2000), Mucci (2013), and Apprey (2003, 2014, 2017). This chapter focuses on the perpetrator fragments that reside within *us*. These perpetrator fragments can cause intrapsychic damage, but we *also* reenact them. These reenactments harm the *other* and our own ethical relation to the *other*. The transgenerational literature addresses these fragments while *also* minimizing attention to them.

We are not surprised to find destructiveness deposited in descendants of the *perpetrators* (see Dietrich L. in Chapter 3). What these inheritors do with this burden is one of the greatest problems posed by transgenerational transmission. Do they reenact the path of their forebears? Will they repudiate cruelty? In our literature, these struggles are manifest in children of Nazis (see Bar-On, 1999; Eckstaedt, 1982). Rosenkotter (1982) describes Helmut E., son of a SS officer, beaten by a father who intended to make him "Hard as steel, tough as leather, quick as a gray-hound" (p. 179). Despite, or because of, this abuse, Helmut E. identifies with his father's Nazi ideals. Rosenkotter also describes Werner C., another son of a Nazi, who has an obsessional *fear* that he will kill his beloved 3-year-old child. The *dread* of an inherited

DOI: 10.4324/9781003087762-10

Nazi self is evident in the life of Enola Sielbert (above). This appears in Guralnik's (2014) self-annihilating patient, Nyx, who fears that she has irreparably damaged her own infant by drinking during her pregnancy. Frie (2019) escapes from both extremes: Discovering that his beloved German grandfather was a Nazi takes him on a path of historical revelation and social justice.

In this literature, the persecutor is largely visible through those they have subjugated, who cry out for justice. This is true for the inheritors of the Armenian genocide (see Altounian, 1999; Hachikian, 2017), who still seek global recognition of this genocide. Black analysts have written extensively on the inherited effect of slavery and persecution; reparations still have not arrived (Apprey, 1999; Gump, 2000, 2017; Holmes, 2012; Leary, 2005; Stephens, 2022; Stoute, 2019, 2021; Vaughans, 2015). Some analysts have traced their persecutory whiteness through their transgenerational history (see Grand, 2014, 2018a; Harris, 2012; Woods, 2020).

Why isn't the perpetrator a more direct focus in this literature? This absence is multiply determined. In 2000, Grand suggested that perpetrator parts operate in self-states without depressive concern. These states lack the I–Thou capacity and reflectivity. Most notably, these states lack *historicity*. She theorizes that, in these modalities, the harm done is twinned with the erasure of history, thereby creating a "malignant dissociative contagion." Then, too, as Frie (2019) suggests, familial bonding and cultural mythology makes us deny the perpetrator within our familial history. Kanavou, Path, and Doll (2016) see this in descendants of the Khmer Rouge in the Cambodian genocide. In their compliance with an authoritarian culture, in justifying the actions of their parents, these descendants are primed to repeat genocidal violence if instructed to do so. For descendants of victims, victimization can become a permit for reenacting violence, even as we claim our own innocence. And in Kestenberg's (1982) observations of children of Holocaust survivors, he encounters the fantasy that future victimization can be prevented by becoming Nazi oppressors: "Better to be a Nazi than a Jew." All of these issues make it difficult for us to focus on our perpetrator fragments.

Visibility and Invisibility: Seeing the Perpetrator Object

One cannot overcome an enemy who is absent or not within range. [Trauma] must be recreated not as an event in the past but as a present-day force ... For when all is said and done, it is impossible to destroy anyone in absentia.

Freud (1912, p. 108)

In this chapter, I am arguing that healing requires that we make the perpetrator more *visible*. The transgenerational literature does trace an internalized persecutory object that keeps re-burying both life *and* death in the "crypt" (Abraham & Török, 1994). This process typically focuses on the resultant pain *inside* of us. In this chapter, I argue, with Apprey, that forgotten traumatic history is often evacuated and performed through intrapsychic, interpersonal, and social destruction. To know ourselves as descendants of perpetrators; to discover ourselves enacting some of the perpetrator fragments that haunt our survivor families: These awakenings are often the most painful, and the most denied, aspects of transmission. Can we look at this in ourselves?

As therapists, we focus on the historic persecution that attacks our patient, generations later. As difficult as this work is, it is rooted in *human innocence*. But when our forebears' split-off hatred arrives in the office, it can be incoherent, fragmentary, murderous, suicidal, and shaming. Liner (2017) describes this as an inherited, untranslatable excess, enigmatically communicated by prior generations, partitioned off into a psychotic enclave, then reproduced as cruelty and sadism. When descendants narrate history by turning someone else into an "it," innocence is lost. To decode this, it becomes, as Freud (1917) suggested, "fruitless ... to contradict a patient who brings these accusations against his ego. He must surely be right in some way ... He has lost his self-respect and he must have good reason for this" (pp. 146–147).

This recognition occurs in Volkan's (2017) case of Peter. This successful man worked in the weapons industry. In childhood, Peter's father abandoned him. His stepfather bonded with Peter, saving him from his smothering mother. The stepfather survived the 1942 Bataan death march and Japanese prisoner-of-war camps. When Peter suffered from shame, he would fly a helicopter over a herd of deer and machine gun the animals, watching them explode. Peter discovers that the stepfather gave Peter an unconscious mission: to be a vicious hunter rather than the hunted.

Denial and the Antidote to Denial

We are human, and we whitewash our own transgressions. For Apprey (2014), this denial can ensue when our ancestors have suffered mass violence. Afterwards, there is a very human tendency to "purge ourselves of some inchoate and unmetabolized parts of ourselves—parts of ourselves we dare not admit as belonging to us and must therefore be housed elsewhere" (pp. 6–7). This tendency can ignite our destructiveness, as our unwanted parts are "deposited to the world of *no place*, namely, death of the Other" (p. 7). He continues: "Humans live in the past as well as in the present and what they do with the Other to purify themselves and to render the Other inferior, useless, or dead" (p. 7). This is transmitted to the next generation.

This form of transgenerational repetition is one of the greatest challenges that we meet in the clinical process. As therapists, we can feel like our patients' persecutors if we point out their dissociated enactments of aggression. As patients receiving this feedback from our own analysts, we can feel that our innocence—and that of our persecuted forebears—is being soiled once again. As therapists, we can feel mortified and defensive when our patient sees our own perpetrator fragments.

As therapists, we need to reduce our own resistance to recognizing our own perpetrator fragments. To do this, we need the humanizing container that our trauma theory offers us. This trauma model relies on Ferenczi's insight: The traumatized child *vacates* her own mind and *internalizes* her abuser's reality through an "identification with the aggressor." Our model relies, as well, on Anna Freud's extension of Ferenczi's concept: Identification with the aggressor can operate through *mimicry, externalization,* and *reenactments.* Histories of atrocity can result in an "obstinate attachment" to an inherited "internal saboteur" (see Fairbairn, 1944). Relational trauma theory postulates a psyche at war with, and attached to, multiple internalized objects. The internal saboteur is embedded in splintered self-other configurations. These self–other configurations are thought to be inscribed with positions of perpetrator, bystander, and victim (Davies & Frawley, 1994; Grand, 2000; Howell, 2005). If we link Relational trauma theory to Apprey's concept of the transgenerational errand, we can imagine that our self-states might be engaged with multiple mandates. Some self-states embrace the humane capacities that our forebears gave us; other self-states can be pre-symbolic, narrating persecution through its repetitions. As Grand (2019) notes, these pre-symbolic communications can include, for example, an eroticized idealization of vengeance, inherited not from a *perpetrator,* but rather from a concentration camp liberator. As Moss (2010) suggests, this eroticized violence can be transmitted by an allied World War II soldier, who was fighting "the just war."

As clinicians, we need an open mind about what we are encountering—in ourselves and in our patient. As Stoute (2019, 2021) suggests in her work on surviving racism, there are transgenerational motifs of self-protection, dignity, communal bonding, and the capacity to love despite being hated. One of these motifs is black rage, too often read by white people as dangerous and destructive. When considering signs of destructive repetition, analysts need to reflect on their own social positioning and the lens through which we are looking. In the complex knot of history and culture, in the mutuality of the analytic setting, the actual *meaning* of these dynamisms will unfold more readily *if analysts can recognize their own perpetrator fragments*.

Ethical Labyrinths and Internalized Perpetrators

History can seem like a series of knots: Untie one, and another appears. Many of our forebears navigated shifting epochs and shifting positions within these epochs. Our families may have been oppressed in one context, dominant in another. I, for example, descend from poor Russian Jews who emigrated to the US in flight from pogroms. Those who didn't emigrate died in the Holocaust. In the US, my relatives encountered anti-Semitic hatred and exclusion. But over generations, many poor immigrant Jews moved upwards in class and achieved a provisional whiteness in the US. There has been considerable Jewish solidarity with anti-racist activism. But this "whitening" of American Jews often meant complicity with the anti-black racism which is the foundation of "whiteness" in the US (see Brodkin, 2010). As Layton (2017) describes this, her own American Jewish whiteness answers, "An intergenerationally transmitted imperative held by all four of my grandparents, to escape, via assimilation, the traumas of Eastern European pogroms," intensified by the "Western European associations of Eastern European Jews with dirt, darkness, and American anti-Semitism" (pp. 153–154). Like Bloch (2017), I am scarred by a heritage of victimization and tainted by a heritage of perpetration.

Given the ubiquity and complexity of this kind of history, it is likely that most of us have perpetrator fragments within us. Krondorfer (2016) recommends that we depart from victim/perpetrator labeling; instead, he suggests that we think in terms of "harm done" and "harm endured." We need language for our destructiveness, without foreclosing our humanity or that of our persecuted forebears. For both Apprey (2003) and Volkan (2017), the tasks that survivors deposit in their children can include unconscious demands for violent restitution and revenge. According to Volkan, similar commands are "deposited" in descendants of perpetrators. When the second generation cannot complete these tasks, it continues to occupy subsequent generations. The internalized persecutory object destroys intrapsychic linkages, but it can *also* destroy human links *in the real world*. Prager (2016) notes that inhumane reenactments can repeat, as the persecution of one generation gets acted out by subsequent generations.

Accurate labeling for the perpetrator (or their predatory descendant) can be essential; it provides recognition for victims. But as Gobodo-Madikizela (2016) discovers through her truth and reconciliation work in South Africa, this framing can lock a human being into damnation, foreclosing their remorse and efforts toward repair. The language of victim/perpetrator can actually reify the splitting that originally sponsored violence. And since "most people do not occupy the isolated 'position at the bottom,' that the collective illuminates, but rather, more ambiguous, mixed positions in proximity to different vectors of power" (Rothberg, 2019, p. 37), most of us become implicated in others' suffering. There *are* clear categories of historical guilt and innocence. But, as I noted above, historic guilt *and* historic victimization can be simultaneously written on us. Reflecting on the Native American genocide, Grand (2018a) notes that "Colonization pits us against one another in gradations of privilege, objectification, survival and abjection ... Predatory conquest is brilliant and incisive. It perceives and foments our rivalries, our competitions, our cravings for wealth, status, inclusion" (p. 110).

Similar dynamisms can appear in the therapeutic setting. Often, therapists are the first witness to a patient's inherited shame and dread of their own persecutory parts. Therapist and patient: We can each lock into the "doer-done-to" dynamism described by Benjamin (1988), where we meet across historic enmities, and mutually project, enact, and/or perceive the inherited persecutory fragments emanating from the other (see Frie, 2011; Guralnik, 2014; Liner, 2017). These conflicts appear, as well, in group dialogues between descendants of perpetrators and descendants of victims (see Bar-On, 1999). As patients and as therapists, we need to engage with the full complexity of our histories, even as we distinguish between histories of harm done versus harm endured: These are different contexts in which to examine our perpetrator fragments. While addressing this difficult topic, we advocate for remaining rooted in Butler's (2009) ethical perspective:

> It is crucial to distinguish between (a) that injured and rageful subject who gives moral legitimacy to rageful and injurious conduct, thus transmuting aggression into virtue and (b) the injured and rageful subject who nevertheless seeks to limit the injury that she or he causes, and can do so only through an active struggle with and against aggression. The first involves a moralization of the subject that disavows the violence that it inflicts, while the latter necessitates a moral struggle.
>
> (p. 172)

Harm Done: Transgenerational Illuminations

This literature locates the transmission of destructiveness in the un-metabolized wounds and dissociative states of our forebears. Before proceeding to this literature, it is important to note some problematic assumptions in this work. As Prince (2009) and Richman (2017) note, this literature posits a "survivor syndrome," which is then transmitted to descendants. This is a stereotypic portrait of trauma survival, pathologizing survivors, deemphasizing their capacities to live and love, and presuming deficits in their capacity to parent. This portrait *also* assumes that any harm transmitted from survivor to descendant is an *inadvertent, dissociated* product of parental PTSD. This literature does not consider the parent's pre-trauma personality *or* the parent's ongoing social conditions. This literature does not really register the diverse reality of trauma survival. As I review the literature on the transmission of destructiveness, the reader should be mindful of the problematic assumptions that are threaded throughout this work.

This inadvertent, dissociative transmission of destructiveness is described by Faimberg (2005). She suggests that traumatized parents can appropriate the "good" for themselves, extruding hated aspects of themselves into the child's mind. Faimberg considers this a form of psychic violence that parallels the violence done to the parent. Kogan (1995) similarly describes a process in which the survivor parent fosters "a permeable membrane between himself and the child; through which he transmits depressive and aggressive tendencies which cannot be contained in himself" (p. 252). This leads us to ask: How might this extruded hate, aggression, and "badness" manifest in the subsequent generations? The literature attends to the harm done by this extrusion: a sense of badness, guilt, and defect that persists in subsequent generations. But in general, the harm done to the child's mind is seen as a *non-agentic*, unconscious byproduct of parental trauma. This extrusion rarely appears, explicitly, as a persecutor fragment *enacted* by the survivor and/or unconsciously co-constructed *with a child* or in their descendants.

Perpetrator Fragments: Love, Hate, and Restitution

Much of this literature, then, is suggestive of a "malignant transformation" (Sullivan, 1953) that can exist in the conduit between survivor and child. If we return to the splitting of good/bad that can occupy parts of the survivor self-system, we can hear this refrain. Mucci (2013) describes one of the most toxic manifestations of this splitting, in which parental survivors actually project their own perpetrator onto their child. Kestenberg and Kestenberg (1982) cite a case in which a Holocaust survivor refers to a child as "a little Hitler," even putting the child's head in an oven. In Mucci's view, this kind of projection is an identification with the aggressor in which the aggressor's worldview is superimposed on the survivor's intimate object relations. Laub and Auerhahn (1993) have also pointed to a milder projection onto children after the Holocaust, where the child's individuation can be conflated, by survivor parents, with forced separation and with their persecutor's cruelty.

To better understand these projective phenomena, we might turn to Abraham and Török's (1994) theory of transmission, in which the incorporated abusive object gets relocated onto an indigestible foreign object; this can be the survivor's *own child and their descendants*. Thus, as Kogan (1995) suggested, instead of acting as a protective shield, the parent creates a permeable membrane with the child, through which they transmit aggressive tendencies that cannot be contained within the parent. For Laub and Auerhahn (1993) and Newirth (2016), this projection is a miscarriage of symbolization in the survivor.

Mucci (2013), however, was pointing to the most destructive form of transfer: a malignant and paranoid percept of the child. What is the intrapsychic and interpersonal fate of this projection? Let's think about the suicidal, self-attacking, and/or murderous enactments this projection might incite: What does this look like? For some clarification, we turn again to Newirth (2016), as he distinguishes between two paranoid-schizoid modes that may haunt survivors, affecting the next generation. He refers to the *passive* paranoid-schizoid form of being-in-the-world that is familiar to us in states of powerlessness and self-attack inside survivors and their descendants. Newirth also proposes a more *active* form of paranoid-schizoid process in survivors: an aggressive defensive mode. Denying fear and dependency, this mode is akin to Klein's manic defense. Contemptuous, power-seeking, and grandiose, this is an idealization of the destructive parts of the self (see also Richards, 2018).

In this *active* paranoid defense, a perverse form of agency is attributed to survivors who conflate their children with the enemy. This agentic paranoid defense characterizes the fathers of Moss (2010) and Grand (2019) as they repeat violent war stories. Here, the child is asked to admire the father's violence, join with his sadism, and eroticize his violence. This is an unconscious mandate to protect *the father from feeling terror and grief.* Amir (2016) suggests that the result of this can be that "the child turns the grave in which he or she had been buried alive into a false psychic space where any dialogue is immediately altered into a kind of tyrannical power struggle" (p. 542). Like many analysts writing about transgenerational legacies, Amir does not elucidate the fate of this "tyrannical power struggle" in the next generation, but we can imagine what might come next. Enlisted in an idealized identification with parental violence, keeping faith with the manic defenses of parents, and filled with their own childhood pain, descendants may renew domination, aggression, subjugation.

Perverse Forms of Reparation: Loneliness and Eros

Silence in our forebears can *also* morph into predatory fantasies/enactments in the next generation. Here, as Grand (2000), Mucci (2013), and Salberg (2017) suggest, children's unconscious fantasies elaborate the unspoken trauma story. Parental silence is filled with *menacing* objects; these are shaped by the child's own familial pain. Grand (2000) presents James, a descendant of the Armenian genocide, who claims that he knows nothing of this history. Friendly but concrete, he talks exclusively about his daily life and has a vague air of loneliness. He complained of his wife's disinterest in sexuality and is not interested in his night terrors. In bed, he wanted his wife to enact scenarios of theft, rape, and humiliation. Initially compliant, his wife gradually refused to comply. In sessions, compulsive and degrading erotica were directed toward the analyst; he had no interest in its meaning. Finally, his therapist told him that he could not turn his therapy into sex talk. This replicated his wife's refusal to comply.

This struck James as a recurrent *no* voiced by a woman to her predator; it opened his memories. James grew up with his working-class family: mother, father, and his maternal aunt. The father and aunt went to work during the day. Both the mother and aunt were warmly maternal. But during the day, his mother would shut herself in, weeping. James would sit by the closed door, lonely, mystified, and worried. Eventually, she would emerge without explanation or emotional repair. At night, his mother woke up screaming, and once again, James was shut out. After the analyst's *no*, James reports this: In his early adolescence, he initiated sex with his kindly, maternal aunt. Weeping, she said, "You are like my son. You do this to a mother?" (p. 40). James heard her despair, felt her tears, and removed his hand from her breast. Another secret emerged. As a young man, he had passively watched a gang rape in the park. He did nothing for the rape victim even after the rapists had fled. Until the analyst's *no*, these episodes were dissociated and unmarked by guilt or shame. Through these memories, James discovered his unconscious story about female forebears during the genocide: He had imagined them as *willing girls in erotic play with predators*. In his fantasy life, James substituted erotic arousal for the terror of genocide and rape. In James' childhood, his otherwise nurturing mother would recurrently disappear, weeping during the day and screaming in the night. Where was she? Who and what was haunting her? Why wasn't she there for him? At night, mother and aunt would weep together. To James, they would not speak. In adolescence, there was a surge of erotic need *and* of "catastrophic loneliness." In his hurt, abandonment, and rage, he unconsciously identified with their rapists. Better to be a genocidal Turk than a bereft, helpless boy; better to bond with their perpetrator than to have no one.

Reflecting on this case now, I wonder if this enactment was unconsciously co-constructed in this traumatized family. In the traumatized, there is an urgent need for remorse and recognition from the perpetrator (see Herman, 2023). This longing inspired Ensler's (2019) *The Apology*, in which she writes the apology that she will never receive from her predatory father. In the conduit between survivor and descendant, in the familial unconscious, there may be a craving for a "reparative perpetrator phantasm." In this fantasy, the perpetrator re-turns, his predation is visible; the victim's voice of *no* is heard, and the perpetrator arrests his crime and sees the wound that he has wrought. Perhaps, in this way, James enacted the "reparative perpetrator phan-tasm" by initiating incest with his aunt, feeling her tears, heeding her *no*, and removing his hand from her breast.

In my view, this reparative perpetrator phantasm can exist in a fam-ily as a deadly *and* exciting object (Fairbairn, 1944) that *also* inscribes history. But enacting this fantasy does *not* bring reparation; it ruptures trust and reopens the original wound. Fonagy (1999b) described work-ing with a 10-year-old boy whose sadistic sexual fantasies seemed linked to a history of his grandmother's sexual slavery during the Holo-caust. These cases illustrate a perverse form of testimony, an imaginary undoing of history, and an infliction of the history that needs undoing.

These enactments echo another imaginary that Liotti (2004) sug-gests may reside in the next generation: a fantasy of being the savior of both the survivor *and* the persecutor. As Neri (2016) would put this, descendants are interpolated into familial history and into familial fan-tasy about that history. The descendant, like James, can become his forebears' "unspeakable monster" (p. 409). From Grand's perspective, this unspeakable monster renews historic violation, even as it attempts an unconscious answer to an unconscious hunger for restitution.

Displacement and False Repositories: Who Is the Historic Enemy?

Maurice Apprey has offered us the most thorough and courageous reckoning with our inherited destructiveness. His work asks how re-ceived hatred is transformed and misdirected through generations, par-ticularly in black descendants of African American slavery. Apprey is interested in the way that history is both ruptured and stored in cultural memory. He explores what injured communities put into the residual wound. How do they fill an absence? Like Liner (2017), Apprey sug-gests that history is often taken in through *intromission*, a process that forecloses more conscious, agentic efforts to transform (or effectively repress) the injury. Intromission makes the injury resistant to change because it cannot be translated into the symbolic present.

Here, deadly secrets are injected by an ancestral object through the transmission of destructive aggression (Apprey, 2014). The perpetrator has installed atrocity inside slavery's descendants, so that contemporary

African Americans must house ancestral figures who are in continual war: the ghost of a slave-master, and the ghost of a slave who is raped, tortured, or killed. The slave-master is internalized as a saboteur, an internal assassin, demanding some form of self-destruction. Children's minds are the receptors for inchoate errands intended to repair history. Apprey (2014) observes that the intromission of history changes functions through the generations. The errand can manifest as destructiveness in one generation, suicide in the next. For descendants who receive a more *symbolic* errand from their forebears, there are more constructive, non-destructive, forms of inscription and repair. In either condition, the errand is injected from an anterior source, housed in a timeless and deferred state, to be carried out "by the subject for an internal object" (p. 17).

Too often, in the aftermath of mass violence, Apprey (2003) observes that there is a "mandate to preserve the originary legacy of ashes in new but equally destructive forms" (p. 9). This mandate is "striving to repeat historical injury, choosing an inappropriate object to attack during the repetition, and haphazardly repeating the errand toward extinction or haphazardly re-creating a wayward child" (p. 15). For Apprey, the occlusion of history results in losing sight of the real historic enemy, even as there is an urgent need to find and punish this enemy. This can result in destructive displacements, in which the urge for retribution and justice finds its enemy in the wrong object. Thus, the mandate for restitution and justice can proceed unfulfilled through the generations. The result can be an ever-renewed dynamism. The descendant who is the recipient of this mandate will, in loyalty to their forebears, seek an object for punishment and for the extrusion of badness. Individuals, families, and collectives can then lose sight of who sent whom on this errand. The errand itself remains inchoate and untranslated. Elaborating the *events of history* through a misdirected *sense of history*, violence and destructiveness can be misdirected toward oneself, one's family, one's own group, or another oppressed group. This kind of repetition is exemplified in Hassinger's (2014) case of Edwin. This analysis is a dialogue between a white, female therapist and a black man who, as a child, was subjected to brutal discipline by his older sisters. Edwin shows Hassinger a photo from the 1930s, in which a young black man is stripped and about to be whipped by a white guard.

I keep coming back to this picture and the sensation that I'd been there, that I was that boy. I realize that the way he is standing, with his trousers pulled down and his hands held behind his back, is exactly how I had to stand during the whippings I received as a kid. My grandpa was the coach. He was a stupid and cruel man. He told my sisters how to do it. He'd say, "This is how they whipped 'em into shape when I was a boy." You know grandpa was born just before the emancipation.

(p. 351)

To end this cycle of violence, Apprey (2003) wants to give the internal assassin a "decent burial, knowing that the phantom is part of the self and cognizant that the ghost may return if one is not vigilant or resilient" (p. 15).

Psychoanalysis Itself: Transgenerational Legacies of Harm Done

A critical review of the transgenerational literature on destructiveness could stop here. But to arrest the recycling of harm done, we must *also* address psychoanalysis itself. Our own discipline is not just a forum for healing; it has also been a transgenerational site of *harm done* in the areas of race, ethnicity, class, gender identity, sexual orientation, and gendered violence. Throughout the history of our discipline, analysts have illuminated these problems and offered correctives. Much praise has been devoted in this text to our healing effects. But our theory and practice are still infused with perpetrator fragments inherited from our forebears' problematic culture. As Frosch (2019) notes, "the violence of the social is an iterative one, expressed as norms that are constantly repeated in order to counter the subject's intrinsic capacity to resist" (pp. 68–69).

Despite our best efforts, these problems get repeated within this text. The literature itself is primarily white and Western. We, the authors, can't read anything but English. What Big Histories gain entry to this text? What "qualifies" as psychoanalytic? Whose trauma matters? Our discipline has held universalist assumptions and pathologizing presumptions and imposed them on women, the non-Western, the non-normative, the non-white. Maurice Apprey (2003) works across cultures with violent histories. He acknowledges *both* our good faith intentions *and* our damaging presumptions. He calls for us to disclose our basic assumptions and to embrace an "ethic of translation":

The recognition that ideas can *carry over* from one place to another, sometimes well, sometimes badly. It is the recognition that the formulation of theory can also *betray* those whom we wish to describe.

These two meanings—translation as a carrying over and translation as betrayal—require us to be extremely careful as clinicians, researchers, and theorists … our theoretical formulations should always be thought of as provisional and idiomatic, never wholly satisfactory. We must ensure that our theoretical formulations do not injure the other.

(p. 5)

Even as analysts widen the scope of our transgenerational literature, universalizing assumptions and exclusions persist at the core of analytic theory (see Grand, 2018b). These assumptions evolved in bourgeois, 19th-century Vienna. It is difficult for us to learn from, or speak with, cultures that are rooted in extended family, communal values and attachments, less preoccupied by wealth production, more immersed in nature, and linked to the spiritual world. Our theory is not built to accommodate these differences. The tendency has been *either* to neglect other cultures with their Big Histories or to pathologize/occlude difference. To be read into psychoanalysis, *non-Western* culture has been forced to assimilate into "our" constructs. Given these inherent limitations, it can be difficult for many Big Histories to even enter our canon.

Exclusions and Restorations of Big History

What is being included in this volume, and what might be invisibly excluded? It can be difficult to witness some of the damage caused by our universalist discourse unless we turn to Big Histories that are marginalized by psychoanalysis. Yael Danieli's (1998) edited text provides the reader with an expansive embrace of cultures and histories. Here, we find literature that does not appear in strictly psychoanalytic venues. This text offers a more inclusive look at indigenous genocides, at the colonial violence suffered by the Global South, at wars and atrocities generally overlooked by Western psychoanalysis: the Japanese internment during World War II in the US; the atomic bomb survivors of Japan; the Cambodian genocide; the Turkish genocide of the Armenians; the wars in Yugoslavia and in southeast Asia; state terror in South America; the colonization trauma of Australian aborigines; American chattel slavery; and the traumatic heritage of the First Peoples in the US. This inclusive effort was continued in two texts on transgenerational transmission edited by the co-authors (Grand & Salberg, 2015; Salberg & Grand, 2017). In Danieli's compendium, these Big Histories are suddenly visible; we find respect for non-Western traditions, family structures, and healing practices. These articles are *not* written *about* the *subjects* of these inheritances; they are written *by* these inheritors. Many analysts would dismiss these culturally embedded articles as "psychology"; too often, this term seems to denote something inferior to "depth" psychoanalysis.

Listening to the Harm Done

For a brilliant critique of this racialized Western supremacy in psychoanalysis, I turn to Duran, Duran, Brave Heart, and Horse Davis (1998). They address the transgenerational "soul wound" of their Lakota peoples in the US in the long aftermath of the indigenous genocide. For these authors, this "soul wound" emanates from being literally and culturally annihilated, from being forced into a "colonial lifeworld, where the Native lifeworld was despised and thought of as inferior and evil" (p. 344). This echoes and repeats in new iterations over the centuries, so that colonial paternalism and destruction is never situated in the past. In articulating the transgenerational effects of their American Holocaust (see Stannard, 1992), they find resonance with Kestenberg's (1990) Western psychodynamic formulation of "survivor's child complex" in descendants of the Holocaust, as does Brave Heart (1998), who also finds resonance with Fogelman's (1991) depiction of mourning trouble in Holocaust survivors. Echoing the Holocaust literature, Brave Heart refers to the difficulty mourning a mass grave, expressing collective grief, particularly when survivors must live among the perpetrators and murderers of their families. Thus, these authors make creative use of Western psychoanalytic formulations. Nonetheless, they still challenge and distrust the colonial worldview inherent in these Western formulations:

> Behavioral theories decontextualize and individualize social problems and many sociocultural theories continue European representations of native peoples that have origins in the politics of the colonial and early American era. Insofar as these approaches are cultural products ... we can say that they are hegemonic. By this we mean that they partake in ideological/cultural domination by the assertion of universality and neutrality and by the disavowal of all other cultural forms or interpretations.
>
> (Duran et al., 1998, p. 353)

Following that line of thinking, Duran et al. (1998) regard Western therapies as continuing to colonize the Lakota lifeworld. To repair the "soul wound," healing practice must recognize colonial destructiveness and restore the Lakota lifeworld. Instead of PTSD, the authors rewrite the diagnostic category for their "soul wound" to "Chronic and Acute Reactions to Colonialism" (p. 347). Referencing Villanueva (1989), they agree that the problems facing these communities can only be ameliorated if "responsibility is placed in the right place" (p. 30). With this clarity, Duran et al. (1998) suggest that the violence and suicide that plagues descendants of First Peoples should be reframed as Curry (1972) did: "The explicit and conscious act of killing involves the affirmation of life, which is nourished by that which is killed ... The patient [is] only killing an image of himself" (p. 103)—that is, he is killing the devalued self-image internalized from the perpetrator.

Addressing Harm Done

As I noted above, this transgenerational work is hard to find in our psychoanalytic journals. Any review of the *analytic* literature on transgenerational transmission must recognize that psychoanalysis was written as a patriarchal, Western, Enlightenment project. In psychoanalysis, we have often neglected the unique sociopolitical context in which trauma is endured and from which it is transmitted (see Brickman, 2017; Grand, 2018b).

This critique has been acknowledged by Mucci (2013), but it is best articulated by LaCapra (2002) and Rothberg (2008). To these authors, we have been homogenizing historical trauma, so that the trauma of "others" is assimilated to "our" worldview and culture, mirroring "our" war. Cournut (2010) alerts us to this truth: "Psychoanalysis comes close to the indictment of irrelevance to the extent that it claims to hold a universal discourse about the human being based on a highly specific experience of recent and disputed invention" (p. 605). This tendency has been resisted in the work of Lazali (2018) and Wikinski (2018) on colonial trauma in Algeria and Argentina, who trace similarities while also clarifying cultural differences. The homogenization of trauma is also resisted in Krondorfer's (2016) intercultural work with opposing descendants of the Holocaust. Krondorfer calls for us to be conscious of our embeddedness in our group's history and asks us to greet the trauma of others with an "empathic unsettlement" that does not contrive similarity or imagine closure. This call is key to relinquishing the biases written into this literature. As we relinquish those biases, our capacity to witness expands.

Transgenerational Figures and Figurations in My Representational World

Maurice Apprey, Ph.D.*: Personal Story

There are multiple *figures* that feature prominently in my representational world. There is the *figure* of a discreet grandfather who taught *strategy* to freedom fighters in their bid to gain independence from the British in the Gold Coast, now Ghana. There is the *figure* of a grandmother who was so authoritative and powerful that her ten sons nicknamed her Mr. Araba. There is the figure of my mother who taught that "when your job is large you do it all" (sic). There is the *figure* of a father who had a smile even in the face of adversity. These are the key *dramatis personae* of my internal life.

The *figuration*, and contributions, of these *external fields of reference to my internal life* continue to keep me at work psychically. Grandfather was the one who would tap me on the shoulder and say: "Grandma is not in a good mood today. Be sure to stay out of trouble," or "It is quiet here today. I have new tennis balls in the storage room. Fetch them and go and play with your friends." To this I would respond: "I am quite happy sitting here *alone with you* as you read your newspapers." Accordingly, I knew about the capacity to be *alone with another* inside and outside me before I read Winnicott and loved the resonance between lessons I learned developmentally and those that came later in life.

Grandmother could both discipline and give aim and direction. My mother's yeoman-like attitude to life has served me well. I can easily identify an ego identification with her and recall a period in my life when I was practicing child analysis, adult analysis, participating in ethno-national conflict resolution in the Baltics after the breakdown of the Soviet Union, teaching and supervising psychiatric residents in Virginia, and teaching psychoanalytic candidates in Istanbul and

DOI: 10.4324/9781003087762-11

Washington, as well as serving in various Deanship positions in a Research 1 University.

My father's smile joins the combined resilience-training camp, as it were, built with the infrastructure of my grandparents' and mother's legacy. This is why I could find a way to grieve and work analytically, and productively, when my late wife was killed by a hit-and-run driver two decades ago. The work of growing and working productively continues.

Horizontally, the link between grandfather and grandmother gives me the *bold discretion* I need to work collaboratively and/or fight in the academy that is replete with competing or hostile interests, and to undertake bold initiatives as a Dean for African Americans in a University that was originally built by slaves to create future American leaders, that is, Caucasian men. I have been at the forefront of successfully fostering integration and making substantive changes for four decades.

Vertically, and transgenerationally, whereas my grandfather discreetly mentored nationalists and others, I became a tenured full professor and psychoanalyst who fostered a restructuring of minds *behind closed doors*.

Palpably, what then was my errand?

Note

* Maurice Apprey, Ph.D., D.M., FIPA, is Professor of Psychiatry Emeritus at the University of Virginia.

6

Social Justice
Conflict Resolution and Transgenerational Studies

Sue Grand

> History, like trauma, is never simply one's own ... history is pre-
> cisely the way we are implicated in each other's trauma.
>
> (Caruth, 1995, p. 24)

Most of this volume is devoted to the wound that arrives in
psychoanalysis. This intimate reckoning is essential, but it will never
be enough. For every individual in psychotherapy, thousands—nay,
millions—are subjected to mass trauma. In large-scale political conflicts, transgenerational dynamisms are ever-present. Within and
between groups, ancient wounds find expression through renewed destruction. Big Histories of malignant trauma appear in every chapter
of this book and cry out for psychic *and* cultural repair, even as new
epochs of violence are being ignited. Can societies arrest these cycles
of violence by putting their ancient ghosts to rest? Can the transgenerational lens facilitate this process? Collective ghosts, un-mourned
histories, recycled violence, memorialization, and the search for conflict resolution: This is the focus of Vamik Volkan, Maurice Apprey,
Gobodo-Madikizela, and others. Our final chapter focuses on these
large-group processes.

An ethos of social responsibility is implicit in the transgenerational
literature. The problem of othering is a general motif. Psyche and
culture are viewed as intertwined, and culture emerges as an "ethical
labyrinth." Reading this literature, it becomes clear that some of us
live *in a humane and lawful world*, while others are excluded from it.
Too often, group/familial cohesion seems to rely on finding a "monstrous double" (Girard, 1977) in the Other, exploited, abused, and cast
as a malignant invasion. To purge the body politic, violence toward

DOI: 10.4324/9781003087762-12

the Other is often sanctioned. It is noteworthy that most persecutory regimes regard themselves as *victims* of the Other, so that aggression is legitimized as justice. In our view, this is an inversion of truth and a perversion of justice; it is another form of violence. In Volkan's (2017) transgenerational perspective, this kind of system is an "entitlement ideology" that seeks restitution for a culture's *open wounds*. These ancient wounds can refer back centuries, to a lost war, colonization, the assassination of beloved leaders, genocide, epochs of famine, forced migration, and so on. Entitlement ideologies do not attempt to heal these wounds; rather, they exploit this history, asserting compensatory rights to wealth, domination, and aggression. For those who are elevated in these entitlement ideologies, the oppression of others is seductive:

> It is not even that these mechanisms of rationalization are *available*, it is also that they are, at times, *irresistible:* the world turns around them, violence is the draw, and the technique and the moral virtue; without it we fear being trodden into the ground.
>
> (Frosch, 2019, p. 68)

Too often, culture recycles ancient injuries in repetitions of aggression and dehumanization. But cultures can also pursue forms of memorialization and justice that put these ghosts to rest. In doing so, culture can act as Benjamin's (2004) *moral third*: a lawful, humane world in which every person's dignity is respected and losses can be mourned. Restoring the *moral third* for the abject requires public forums for reparation, testimony, and witnessing (Gobodo-Madikiezela, 2016; Volkan, 2017). In these forums, there is *no* witness who can stand *outside* of the shared social realm. In agreement with Rothberg (2019), Frosch (2019) refers to all of us as "implicated witnesses" and recognizes the loop of violence that we need to break out of:

> Historical, colonial, and political violence—used in racialized and gendered forms—feed off and into the violence in which subjects are "mired" and the violence in which subjects are mired is incited to support the ends of those who advance historical, colonial, and political violence.
>
> (p. 69)

Hamburger (2018) is a German analyst working in the aftermath of the Holocaust. His descriptions of cultural processes resonate with those of Frosch and Apprey:

> Social trauma is executed in a societal context, thus involving the surrounding society in the traumatic process, printing the cliché of victim and perpetrator on the whole group. It results in a process of group victimization, but also of "perpetratorization."
>
> (p. 110)

For these authors, the unmetabolized *collective* past inscribes both re-victimization and re-perpetration of large-group processes. We reenact history because history has never been collectively recognized and mourned. As we discussed earlier, ghosts cannot be put to rest without this witnessing. In addition to individual witnessing within analysis, we need the collective witnessing of *both* our wounds *and* our violence. Walker (2016) believes that this collective witnessing helps us to relinquish the fixed, rigid group identities that characterize intractable conflict. For Walker, when our group identities are more flexible, we are more inclined toward peaceful cultural transformation, which requires the *cultural* enhancement of our intersubjective capacities. At a large-group level, this refers to the ability "to see yourself as others see you while not dissociating the experience of how you see yourself" (Bromberg, 2006, p. 331). Unfortunately, cultures seem proficient at constructing an "us versus them" psychology, but our collectives can also construct its antidote: Fromm's (1958) "revolutionary character" is concerned with the dignity of all of humanity. In their study of historic wounds and group conflict, Pivnick and Hassinger (2023) issue a call for "relational citizenship." If collectives could make these shifts, *real contemporary dangers* would not inflame ancient wounds. Group activation and reactivity would be reduced; responses to actual danger would be more life-affirming and considered. Othering would lessen. This is the goal of psychoanalysts applying the transgenerational lens to large conflicts.

Ancient Trauma, Open Wounds: Recycling Violence

Volkan (e.g., 2017) has worked extensively across cultures in pursuit of conflict resolution and emphasized the large-group identities through which we all define ourselves. To Volkan, these identities remain in the background of our lives until something threatens the group's security. At this writing, for example, global citizens have lived through the intense few years of the COVID-19 pandemic and are now feeling threatened by climate change, refugee crises, neo-fascism, economic uncertainty, and a general sense of precarity. Everyone's security is threatened; millions can become preoccupied with protecting their large-group identity. According to Volkan, they can become willing to do almost anything to repair, protect, and maintain the group. This includes extreme sadism or masochism if they think this will protect their large-group identity. At these times, minor differences within the group become major concerns. Violence and subjugation can be turned outwards toward the external world, but it can also be turned inwards, toward those who signify these minor differences.

Volkan's (2017) theory is a transgenerational approach to these breakdowns. He argues that large-group identity coheres around "specific realistic and/or mythologized past historical events and heroes and martyrs associated with them. Such historical events can be categorized as glorified or traumatic; usually they are both" (p. 147). Volkan refers to these events as "chosen traumas" and "chosen glories." No one, of course, chooses trauma. However, groups share a mental representation of historic trauma, in which humiliation, loss, and helplessness were endured at the hands of the enemy. This can refer to a lost war, to terrorist attacks, genocide, colonization, enslavement, to the assassination of revered figures, and so on. Cultures can nominate these events as central to group history and identity. Because of this centrality to group identity, the historical trauma is kept alive as an open wound. Large groups can dwell upon these events for centuries. Keeping ancestors' traumas alive is often a core task of the group; it consolidates group cohesion. This task is carried forward through generations, a locus of nationalism. A chosen glory is a shared representation of pride in the past: its victories, its achievements, and its heroes. Sometimes, these are intertwined. Groups explicitly celebrate their chosen glories. According to Volkan, these rituals enhance collective self-esteem and inspire collective ideals. Chosen traumas call upon succeeding generations for restitution, repair and/or revenge. These are the transgenerational "errands" described by Apprey (2014). Often, chosen traumas and chosen glories are entwined in problematic cultural narratives. As Gobodo-Madikiezela (2012) puts it, "National/communal hero and victimhood narratives are nostalgic constructions … clinging to idealized images of the past" (p. 93).

Using examples from Turkey, Estonia, Iraq, and the Balkan wars, Volkan wades into the distant past to find the origins of these chosen traumas. Often, they refer to a humiliating defeat in the *Middle Ages*. Cultures often maintain these memories as *open wounds*; they are not situated in a mourned, relinquished *past*. These open wounds are readily reignited by charismatic leaders. Linking contemporary stressors to historic humiliation, authoritarian leaders foment violent calls for restitution. The affective aspects of these traumas can remain dormant for long periods of group security. But even when this group affect is dormant, entitlement ideologies insist on undoing historic humiliation and on the recovery of what was lost. In these contexts, restoring what was "lost" usually means reclaiming privilege and domination. For Volkan, this violent insistence reflects a deficit in communal mourning, an inability to reconcile with irreparable loss and to move forward in time. These regimes are organized around a fragile group narcissism. They are organized, as well, by hostile Othering. For Volkan, these structures are both suicidal and murderous, destroying themselves as they make war on the Other. Volkan works with groups in conflict to arrest these cycles. He calls for collective rituals of mourning to narrate history, mourn historic losses, and ameliorate collective humiliation and rage. All of this resonates with the perspective of Apprey, whom we previously reviewed.

As US citizens, the co-authors are daily witnesses to this destructive political theater. Mass shootings are ubiquitous, children are being killed in schools, while the forces of White supremacy insist on their "freedom" to own assault rifles. In the United States, there are more guns than people. Without reference to our colonial history of white indentured servitude and the racing of chattel slavery, it is impossible to make sense of this violence. But if we refer back to the colonial era, we can begin to understand this link between white freedom and gun rights. In the colonial era, labor was brutal. To prevent alliances and effective rebellions between African, European, and indigenous peoples, planters created arbitrary categories of race. Granting some social privileges to poor white indentured servants, inciting their animosity toward their black cohorts, whites were awarded a gun when they were finally granted their freedom. Guns enabled hunting and self-protection. As a marker of white dominance, they were also used to vent humiliated rage at the racialized Other. Guns were never permitted in the hands of black slaves or black free people. In the United States, this abject pre-history of indentured servitude has been erased from white American nationalism, but its visceral aftermath seems to remain as positive proof of

Alford's assessment that "The Western idea of freedom is a defense against narcissistic humiliation" (Drichel, 2018, p. 361).

The erasure of white enslavement means that whiteness has no memory of its own enslavement *with* black and indigenous slaves, no memory of affiliation, kinship, mutual care, and mutual rebellion before slavery was raced (see also Gump, 2010, 2017). Gaztambide (2019), referring to the Harlem Renaissance activist William Pickens, writes that:

> Pickens theorized that "whites have repressed their historical amity with blacks," arguing that a super-ego "watch-dog" stood between conscious hatred and unconscious libido (love), dissociating affective ties to their fellow humans based on the color of their skins, replacing them with "abnormal behaviors, such as mob violence and lynching."
>
> (p. 91)

This flight from, and antidote for, the memory of white indentured servitude not only explains the failure of empathy toward black slavery, as Gump (2017) suggests; it also helps explain the fervor of American gun culture. This forgotten colonial history has been layered onto another epoch of chosen traumas and chosen glories: the American Civil War of the mid-19th century. This war was fought between the anti-slavery North and the pro-slavery South; the North won, and slavery was outlawed. The plantation economy was decimated. The South is still marked by its humiliating loss and by myths of its heroic and noble cause. White supremacy is still flying the confederate flag from that war and insisting that "the South will rise again." In this history, there is an ever-ready lodestone of humiliation and entitled rage, which foments the Neo-Nazi turn in American democracy.

These conditions are unique to white American's history, but their structure is familiar to us all over the world. Phallic violence as an antidote to a chosen trauma and as a resurrection of chosen glories: This has assailed indigenous populations and contributed to the killing of the Rohingya in Myanmar, the persecution of Muslims in India, and the Russian war on Ukraine.

Open Wounds and the Transgenerational Future

If Apprey, Volkan, and others look to the transgenerational past to explicate contemporary violence, Gobodo-Madikizela (2012, 2016) looks at recent enactments to predict a violent transgenerational *future*. This author is a black South African psychologist who worked with the Truth and Reconciliation Committee. Observing girls in a township that suffered from apartheid, the author witnessed this transmission *in vivo* (Gobodo-Madikizela, 2016). In that brutal regime, black resisters were assassinated and tortured. In response to this, those who were accused of being police informers were met with mob justice. Gasoline was poured on a tire; it was wrapped around the neck of the accused, then set on fire. The crowd would dance around the burning body of the informer, some singing until the victim died. These "necklace murders" occurred in the 1980s; this epoch was over before these girls were born. In 1996, this author watched little girls cavorting and laughing, when their leader started the "necklace" game. Cruelty becomes pleasure and death becomes celebration:

> She flailed her arms, screamed in mock anguish as if being pushed around and beaten by an imaginary crowd, swaying back and begging for mercy with eyes wide open to show mock fright. Then she switched roles and playacted someone going off to find petrol, then another person offering matches … As make-believe flames engulfed her, she threw her arms wildly into the air. "Now, sing and clap your hands and dance, I'm dying," she said. Her friends started clapping in a discordant rhythm around her "body." Gradually, the high-pitched screams of the girl ebbed away. Consumed by the flames, she slowly lowered herself to the ground and "died."
>
> (pp. 1–2)

Here, Godobo-Madikizela observes these girls performing cruelty as testimony to their forebears' *unknown* trauma. She grieves, imagining a future scarred by hatred and violence. What she is anticipating, Apprey and Volkan both examined retrospectively. Psychoanalytically informed, working at the repetitive edge of conflict, these authors attempt to heal history.

On Hope and Repairing History

These authors join a multitude of psychodynamic practitioners committed to social justice. For Apprey, Volkan, and Gobodo-Madkizela, the transgenerational lens provides a singular emphasis. This is the need for collectives to narrate their historical traumas, *not as open wounds that demand redress*, but rather through processes of memorialization and mutual care which facilitate *mourning*. This mourning process allows for a group identification that is not defined by chosen traumas and entitlement ideologies. This would reduce our tendency to project our historic enemy onto a contemporary Other. This is the work that Volkan has done around the world. When this collective mourning occurs, it is easier for cultures to enhance intersubjectivity in its citizenry, and to recognize, and care for, those it has persecuted. For Gobodo-Madikizela (and for many others), these cultural shifts must be embedded in creative reckonings with those who have inflicted harm. These creative reckonings might include rigorous empathy toward those who have committed harm, as well as an acknowledgment of our own complicity in violence as Walker (2016) suggests.

For too long, Western justice systems have been strictly rooted in retributive justice. These are penal systems in which the law imposes (or too often, fails to impose) punishment through incarceration or a death sentence. These systems are rarely just. As Herman (2023) notes, these systems have little regard for the needs of the victim and often fail the powerless. Retributive justice systems are not concerned with the moral repair of the perpetrator or with the social health of collectives. As James Gilligan (1996) notes, too often, carceral conditions evoke shame, not guilt, and shame re-ignites violence. Gobodo-Madikizela and many others call for more flexible forms of transitional and transformative justice. These forms of justice are centered on the voice and needs of victims (Herman, 2023). They call for acts of reparation, trying to open up guilt and remorse in the perpetrator. Gobodo-Madikizela advocates for what Brooks (2019) calls an "atonement model":

> Atonement, however, entails much more than the tender of an apology. It also requires making restitution—that is, providing a reparation or reparations commensurate with the atrocity. Reparations are essential to atonement because they make apologies believable. They turn the rhetoric of apology into a meaningful, material reality, and thus, help to repair the damage caused by the atrocity and ensure that the atrocity will not be repeated.
>
> (pp. 142–143)

These efforts emphasize accountability without extruding or dehumanizing the perpetrator. If this works, it is a prophylactic against vengeance. These systems of justice are in the experimental phase around the world. These experiments do not necessarily replace incarceration for those who really require it, but they would greatly decrease incarceration. These are radical turns, particularly for Western cultures. But they hold out hope that we can repair history and be freed from its repetitions. To do this work, to heal the world, we need psychodynamic activists informed by the transgenerational lens.

References

Abraham, N. & Török, M. (1994). *The shell and the kernel: Renewals of psychoanalysis* N. Rand (Ed. & Trans.). University of Chicago Press.

Ainsworth, M. D. (1982). Attachment: Retrospect and prospect. In C. M. Parkes & J. Stevenson-Hinde (Eds.), *The place of attachment in human behavior* (pp. 3–30). Tavistock.

Alpert, J. L. (2001). No escape when the past is endless. *Psychoanalytic Psychology*, *18*(4), 729–736.

Alpert, J. L. (2017). Enduring mothers, enduring knowledge: On rape and history. In J. Salberg & S. Grand (Eds.), *Wounds of history: Repair and resilience in the transgenerational transmission of trauma* (pp. 149–162). Routledge.

Altounian, J. (1999). Putting into words, putting to rest, and putting aside the ancestors. *International Journal of Psychoanalysis*, *80*(3), 439–448.

Amir, D. (2012). The inner witness. *International Journal of Psychoanalysis*, *93*(4), 879–896.

Amir, D. (2016). Hermetic narratives and false analysis: A unique variant of the mechanism of identification with the aggressor. *Psychoanalytic Review*, *103*(4), 539–549.

Apprey, M. (1999). Reinventing the self in the face of received transgenerational hatred in the African American community. *Journal of Applied Psychoanalytic Studies*, *1*(2), 131–143.

Apprey, M. (2003). Repairing history: Reworking transgenerational trauma. In D. Moss (Ed.), *Hating in the first-person plural* (pp. 3–29). Other Press.

Apprey, M. (2006). Difference and the awakening of wounds in intercultural psychoanalysis. *Psychoanalytic Quarterly*, *75*(1), 73–94.

Apprey, M. (2014). A pluperfect errand: A turbulent return to beginnings in the transgenerational transmission of destructive aggression. *Journal of Free Association*, *66*, 15–28.

Apprey, M. (2017). Representing, theorizing and reconfiguring the concept of transgenerational haunting in order to facilitate healing. In S. Grand & J.

Salberg (Eds.), *Transgenerational trauma and the other: Dialogues across history and difference* (pp. 16–38). Routledge.

Aron, L. (1996). *A meeting of minds: Mutuality in psychoanalysis*. The Analytic Press.

Aron, L. (2003). The paradoxical place of enactment in psychoanalysis: Introduction. *Psychoanalytic Dialogues, 13*, 623–631.

Aron, L. (2006). Analytic impasse and the third: Clinical implications of intersubjectivity theory. *International Journal of Psychoanalysis, 87*, 349–368.

Aron, L. & Starr, K. (2013). *A psychotherapy for the people: Toward a progressive psychoanalysis*. Routledge.

Bacciagaluppi, M. (1993). Ferenczi's Influence on Fromm. In L. Aron & A. Harris (eds.), *The Legacy of Sándor Ferenczi* (pp. 185–198). The Analytic Press.

Balint, M. (1968/1979). *The basic fault: Therapeutic aspects of regression*. Brunner Mazel.

Baranger, W., Baranger, M., & Mom, J. M. (1998). The infantile psychic trauma from us to Freud: Pure trauma, retroactivity and reconstruction. *International Journal of Psychoanalysis, 69*, 113–128.

Bar-On, D. (1999). *The indescribable and the undiscussable: Reconstructing the human discourse after trauma*. Central European University Press.

Bass, A. (2003). "E" enactments in psychoanalysis: Another medium, another message. *Psychoanalytic Dialogues, 13*, 657–675.

Beauvoir, S. de. (1949). *The second sex* (H. M. Parshley, Trans.). Vintage Books.

Beebe, B. & Lachmann, F. M. (2014). *The origins of attachment: Infant research and adult treatment*. Routledge.

Beebe, B., Rustin, J., Sorter, D., & Knoblauch, S. (2003). Symposium on intersubjectivity in infant research and its implications for adult treatment. III. An expanded view of forms of intersubjectivity in infancy and its application to psychoanalysis. *Psychoanalytic Dialogues, 13*(6), 805–841.

Benjamin, J. (1988). *The bonds of love*. Pantheon Books.

Benjamin, J. (2004). Beyond doer and done to: An intersubjective view of thirdness. *Psychoanalytic Quarterly, 73*, 5–46.

Benjamin, J. (2009). A relational psychoanalysis perspective on the necessity of acknowledging failure in order to restore the facilitating and containing features of the intersubjective relationship (the shared third). *International Journal of Psychoanalysis, 90*, 441–450.

Benjamin, J. (2016). Moving beyond violence. In P. Gobodo-Madikizela (Ed.), *Breaking intergenerational cycles of repetition* (pp. 71–60). Creative Commons.

Benjamin, J. (2018). *Beyond doer and done to: Recognition theory, intersubjectivity and the third*. Routledge.

Bergmann, M. S. & Jucovy, M. E. (1982). *Generations of the Holocaust*. Basic Books.

Bloch, O. (2017). Dialogues in no man's land. In S. Grand & J. Salberg (Eds.), *Transgenerational trauma and the other: Dialogues across history and difference* (pp. 120–143.). Routledge.

Boulanger, G. (2008). Witness to reality: Working psychodynamically with survivors of terror. *Psychoanalytic Dialogues, 18*(5), 638–657.

Boulanger, G. (2018). When is vicarious trauma a necessary therapeutic tool? *Psychoanalytic Psychology, 35*, 60–69.

Bowers, M. E. & Yehuda, R. (2016). Intergenerational transmission of stress in humans. *Neuropsychopharmacology, 41*, 232–244.

Bowlby, J. (1965). *Attachment and loss: Attachment* (Vol. 1). Basic Books.

Bowlby, J. (1973). *Separation: Anxiety and anger* (Vol. 2). Basic Books.

Bowlby, J. (1980). *Loss: Sadness and depression* (Vol. 3). Hogarth Press.

Brave Heart, M. Y. H. (1998). The return to the sacred path: Healing the historical trauma response among the Lakota. *Smith College Studies in Social Work, 68*(3), 287–305.

Brave Heart, M. Y. H., Yellow Horse, M., Chase J., Elkins, J., & Altschulz, D. (2017). Historical trauma among indigenous people of the Americas: Concepts, research and clinical considerations. In J. Salberg & S. Grand (Eds.), *Wounds of history: Repair and resilience in the transgenerational transmission of trauma* (pp. 250–267). Routledge.

Brickman, C. (2018). *Race in psychoanalysis: Aboriginal populations in the mind.* Routledge.

Brodkin, K. (2010). *How Jews became white folks and what that says about race in America.* Rutgers University Press.

Bromberg, P. M. (1991). On knowing one's patient inside out: The aesthetics of unconscious communication. *Psychoanalytic Dialogues, 1*, 399–422.

Bromberg, P. M. (2001). *Standing in the spaces: Essays on clinical process, trauma, and dissociation.* The Analytic Press.

Bromberg, P. M. (2003). One need not be a house to be haunted: On enactment, dissociation, and the dread of "not-me"—A case study. *Psychoanalytic Dialogues, 13*, 689–709.

Bromberg, P. M. (2006). *Awakening the dreamer: Clinical journeys.* The Analytic Press.

Bromberg, P. M. (2011). *The shadow of the tsunami and the growth of the relational mind.* Routledge.

Brooks, D. (2019, 7 March). The case for reparations: A slow convert to the cause. *New York Times.*

Bruschweiler-Stern, N., Lyons-Ruth, K., Morgan, A. C., Nahum, J. P., Sander, L. W., Stern, D. N. S., Harrison, A. M., Tronick, E. Z., & The Boston Change Process Study Group. (2010). *Change in psychotherapy: A unifying paradigm.* W. W. Norton.

Buber, M. (1923). *I and thou* (W. Kaufman, Trans.). Charles Scribner and Sons.

Bucci, W. (2007). Dissociation from the perspective of multiple code theory—Part II: The spectrum of dissociative processes in the psychoanalytic relationship. *Contemporary Psychoanalysis, 43*(3), 305–326.

Butler, J. (2009). *Frames of war*. Verso.

Caruth, C. (1995). *Unclaimed experience: Trauma, narrative, and history*. Johns Hopkins University Press.

Coates, S. (2004a). John Bowlby and Margaret S. Mahler: Their lives and theories. *Journal of the American Psychoanalytical Association, 52*, 571–601.

Coates, S. (2004b). The role of maternal state in mediating trauma and resilience in preschool children after September 11. Paper presented to the Jewish Board of Family and Children Services.

Coates, S. (2012). The child as traumatic trigger: Discussion of Laurel Silber's "Ghostbusting transgenerational processes." *Psychoanalytic Dialogues, 22*, 123–128.

Coates, S. (2016). Can babies remember trauma? Symbolic forms of representation in traumatized infants. *Journal of the America Psychoanalytic Association, 64*, 751–776.

Cournut, J. (2010). Poor men—or why men are afraid of women. In D. Birksted-Breen, S. Flanders, & A. Gibeault (Eds.), *Reading French psychoanalysis* (pp. 601–622). Routledge.

Curry, A. (1972). *Bringing of forms*. Dustbooks.

Danieli, Y. (1998). *International handbook of multigenerational legacies of trauma*. Springer.

Davies, J. M. & Frawley, M. G. (1994). *Treating the adult survivor of childhood sexual abuse: A psychoanalytic perspective*. Basic Books.

Davoine, F. (2007). The characters of madness in the talking cure. *Psychoanalytic Dialogues, 17*, 627–638.

Davoine, F. & Gaudillière, J. M. (2004). *History beyond trauma: Whereof one cannot speak, thereof one cannot stay silent*. Other Press.

Derrida, J. (1967). *Of grammatology*. Johns Hopkins University Press.

Douglass, F. (1845). *Narrative of the life of Frederick Douglass*. Anti-Slavery Office.

Drichel, S. (2018). The disaster of colonial narcissism. *American Imago, 75*, 329–364.

Duran, E., Duran, B., Brave Heart, M. Y. H., & Horse-Davis, S. Y. (1998). Healing the American Indian soul wound. In Y. Danieli (Ed.), *The international handbook of multigenerational legacies of trauma* (pp. 341–355). Plenum.

Eckstaedt, A. (1982). A victim of the other side. M. S. Bergman & M. E. Jacovy (Eds.), *Generations of the Holocaust* (pp. 197–229). Basic Books.

Eigen, M. (1996). *Psychic deadness*. Jason Aronson.

Ellenberger, H. (1970). *The discovery of the unconscious: The history and evolution of dynamic psychiatry*. Basic Books.

Ensler, E. (2019). *The apology*. Bloomsbury Publishing.

Epstein, H. (1979). *Children of the Holocaust: Conversations with sons and daughters of survivors*. Putnam.

Faimberg, H. (1996). Listening to listening. *International Journal of Psychoanalysis, 77*, 667–677.

Faimberg, H. (1998). The telescoping of generations: Genealogy of certain identifications. *Contemporary Psychoanalysis, 24*, 99–117.

Faimberg, H. (2005). *The telescoping of generations: Listening to the narcissistic links between generations.* Routledge.

Fairbairn, R. G. (1944). Endopsychic structures considered in terms of object-relationships. In *An object relations theory of the personality* (pp. 82–136). Basic Books.

Fanon, F. (1963/2004). *The wretched of the earth* (R. Philcox, Trans.). Grove Press.

Felman, S. (1995). The return of the voice: Claude Lanzmann's Shoah. In S. Felman & D. Laub (Eds.), *Testimony: Crises of witnessing in literature, psychoanalysis and history* (pp. 204–284). Routledge.

Felman, S. & Laub, D. (1992). *Testimony: Crises of witnessing in literature, psychoanalysis and history.* Routledge.

Ferenczi, S. (1916/1917). Two types of war neuroses. In J. Rickman (Ed.), *Further contributions to the theory and technique of psychoanalysis* (pp. 124–141). Brunner Mazel.

Ferenczi, S. (1926). On the definition of introjection. In M. Balint (Ed.), *Final contributions to the problems and methods of psychoanalysis* (pp. 316–318). Karnac Press.

Ferenczi, S. (1929). The unwelcome child and his death instinct. In M. Balint (Ed.), *Final contributions to the problems and methods of psychoanalysis* (pp. 102–107). Karnac Press.

Ferenczi, S. (1932/1995). *The clinical diary of Sándor Ferenczi* (J. Dupont, Ed. & M. Balint & N. Z. Jackson, Trans.). Harvard University Press.

Ferenczi, S. (1933/1949). Confusion of tongues between the adult and the child. *International Journal of Psychoanalysis, 30*, 225–230.

Fogelman, E. (1991). Mourning without graves. In A. Medvene (Ed.), *Storms and rainbows: The many faces of death* (pp. 25–43). Lilith Press.

Fonagy, P. (1999a). *Attachment theory and psychoanalysis.* Guilford Press.

Fonagy, P. (1999b). The transgenerational transmission of Holocaust trauma: Lessons learned from the analysis of an adolescent with obsessive compulsive disorder. *Attachment and Human Development, 1*(1), 92–114.

Fonagy, P., Gergely, G., Jurist, E., & Target, M. (2005). *Affect regulation, mentalization and the development of the self.* Other Press.

Fox, N. (2021). *After genocide: Memory and reconciliation in Rwanda.* University of Wisconsin Press.

Fraiberg, S., Adelson, E., & Shapiro, V. (1975). Ghosts in the nursery: A psychoanalytic approach to the problems of impaired infant-mother relationships. *Journal of the American Academy of Child and Adolescent Psychiatry, 14*, 387–421.

Freud, S. (1912). The dynamics of transference. In J. Strachey (Ed. & Trans), *The standard edition of the complete psychological works of Sigmund Freud* (Vol. 12, pp. 312–322). Hogarth Press.

Freud, S. (1917). Mourning and melancholia. In J. Strachey (Ed. & Trans), *The standard edition of the complete psychological works of Sigmund Freud* (Vol. 14, pp. 237–258). Hogarth Press.

Freud, S. & Breuer, J. (1895). Studies in hysteria. In J. Strachey (Ed. & Trans), *The standard edition of the complete psychological works of Sigmund Freud* (Vol. 2). Hogarth Press.

Frie, R. (2011). Irreducible cultural contexts: German Jewish experience, trauma and identity in a bilingual analysis. *International Journal of Psychoanalytic Self Psychology, 6*, 136–158.

Frie, R. (2019). History's ethical demand: Memory, denial and responsibility. *Psychoanalytic Dialogues, 29*(2), 122–142.

Fromm, E. (1958). *Psychoanalysis and religion*. Yale University Press.

Frosch, S. (2019). *Those who come after: Postmemory, acknowledgment and forgiveness*. Springer.

Gampel, Y. (2019). Trans-generational fallout. In *The Handbook of Psychoanalytic Holocaust Studies*. Ira Brenner (Ed.). Routledge.

Gaztambide, D. J. (2019). *A people's history of psychoanalysis: From Freud to liberation psychology*. Lexington Books.

Gentile, K. (2017). Collectively creating conditions for emergence. In J. Salberg & S. Grand (Eds.), *Wounds of history: Repair and resilience in the transgenerational transmission of trauma* (pp. 169–188). Routledge.

Gerson, S. (2009). When the third is dead: Memory, mourning, and witnessing in the aftermath of the Holocaust. *International Journal of Psychoanalysis, 90*, 1341–1357.

Gilligan, J. (1996). *Violence*. Putnam.

Gilman, S. L. (1993). *Freud, race and gender*. Princeton University Press.

Girard, R. (1977). *Violence and the sacred*. Johns Hopkins University Press.

Gobodo-Madikizela, P. (2012). Remembering the past: Nostalgia, traumatic memory and the legacy of apartheid. *Journal of Peace Psychology, 18*(3), 252–267.

Gobodo-Madikizela, P. (Ed.). (2016). *Breaking intergenerational cycles of repetition*. Creative Commons.

Goodman, D. (2012). *The demanded self: Levinasian ethics and identity in psychology. Reverberations and traces of the Holocaust*. Duquesne University Press.

Grand, S. (2000). *The reproduction of evil: A clinical and cultural perspective*. The Analytic Press.

Grand, S. (2009). *The hero in the mirror: From fear to fortitude*. Routledge.

Grand, S. (2014). Skin memories: On race, love and loss. *Psychoanalysis, Culture and Society, 19*(3), 232–250.

Grand, S. (2015). Circles of witnessing: On hope and atrocity. *Contemporary Psychoanalysis, 51*(2), 262–275.

Grand, S. (2018a). The other within: White racial shame and the Native American genocide. *Contemporary Psychoanalysis, 54*(1), 84–102.

Grand, S. (2018b). Trauma as radical inquiry. In L. Aron, S. Grand, & J. Slochower (Eds.), *Decentering relational theory: A comparative critique* (pp. 5–27). Routledge.

Grand, S. (2019). Excitations of vengeance: The "we-ness" of history. *Psychoanalytic Dialogues, 29*(2), 143–150.

Grand, S. & Salberg, J. (Eds.) (2015). The evolution of witnessing: Emergent relational trends in Holocaust studies. *Contemporary Psychoanalysis, 51*(2), 185–194.

Green, A. (1972). The dead mother. *Psyche, 47*(3), 205–240.

Grotstein, J. S. (1990). Nothingness, meaninglessness, chaos and the "black hole." *Contemporary Psychoanalysis, 3*, 377–408.

Grubich-Simitis, I. (1984). Extreme traumatization as cumulative trauma: Psychoanalytic investigations of the effects of concentration camp experiences on survivors and their children. *Psychoanalytic Study of the Child, 36*, 415–450.

Gump, J. (2000). A white therapist, an African American patient: Shame in the therapeutic dyad. *Psychoanalytic Dialogues, 10*, 619–632.

Gump, J. (2010). Reality matters: The shadow of trauma on African American subjectivity. *Psychoanalytic Psychology, 27*(1), 42–54.

Gump, J. (2017). The endurance of slavery's traumas and truths. In S. Grand & J. Salberg (Eds.), *Transgenerational transmission and the other: Dialogues across history and difference* (pp. 102–119). Routledge.

Guntrip, H. (1969). *Schizoid phenomena, object relations and the self.* International Universities Press.

Guralnik, O. (2014). The dead baby. *Psychoanalytic Dialogues, 24*(2), 129–145.

Guralnik, O. (2016). Sleeping dogs: Psychoanalysis and the sociopolitical. *Psychoanalytic Dialogues, 26*(6), 665–663.

Hachikian, E. V. (2017). Growing up Armenian. In J Salberg & S. Grand (Eds.), *Wounds of history: Repair and resilience in the transgenerational transmission of trauma* (pp. 268–286). Routledge.

Hamburger, A. (2018). After Babel: Teaching psychoanalysis on a former battlefield—experiences in an international research network. *International Forum of Psychoanalysis, 27*(20), 105–113.

Hammerich, B., Pfafflin, J., Pogany, P., Siebert, E., & Sonntag, B. (2016). Handing down the Holocaust in Germany: A reflection on the dialogue between second generation descendants of perpetrators and survivors. In P. Gobodo-Madikizela (Ed.), *Breaking intergenerational cycles of repetition* (pp. 247–265). Creative Commons.

Harris, A. (2006). Ghosts, unhealable wounds, and resilience: Commentary on papers by Sandra Silverman and Maureen Murphy. *Psychoanalytic Dialogues, 16*, 543–551.

Harris, A. (2007). Analytic work in the bridge world: Commentary on paper by Françoise Davoine. *Psychoanalytic Dialogues, 17*, 659–669.

Harris, A. (2012). The house of difference: White silence. *Studies in Gender and Sexuality, 13*, 197–216.

Harris, A. (2014). Discussion of Slade's "Imagining fear." *Psychoanalytic Dialogues, 24*, 267–276.

Harris, A., Kalb, M., & Klebanoff, S. (2016). *Ghosts in the consulting room: Echoes of trauma in psychoanalysis*. Routledge.

Hassinger, J. (2014). Twenty first century living color: Racialized enactments in psychoanalysis. *Psychoanalysis, Culture and Society, 19*(4), 337–360.

Hedgepeth, S. M. & Saidel, R. G. (2010). *Sexual violence against Jewish women during the Holocaust*. Chicago University Press.

Herman, J. L. (1992). *Trauma and recovery: The aftermath of violence from domestic abuse to political terror*. Basic Books.

Herman, J. L. (2023). *Truth and repair: How trauma survivors envision justice*. Basic Books.

Hesse, E., Main, M., Abrams, K. Y., & Rifkin, A. (2003). Unresolved states regarding loss or abuse can have "second-generation" effects: Disorganized, role-inversion and frightening ideation in the offspring of traumatized non-maltreating parents. In D. J. Siegel & M. F. Solomon (Eds.), *Healing trauma: Attachment, mind, body and brain* (pp. 57–106). Norton.

Holmes, D. (2006). The wrecking effects of race and social class on self and success. *Psychoanalytic Quarterly, 76*(1), 215–236.

Holmes, D. (2012). Racial transference reactions in psychoanalytic treatment. In S. Akhtar (Ed.), *The African American experience: Psychoanalytic perspectives* (pp. 363–375). Jason Aronson.

Holmes, J. (1996). *Attachment, intimacy, autonomy: Using attachment theory in adult psychotherapy*. Jason Aronson.

Hopenwasser, K. (2008). Being in rhythm: Dissociative attunement in therapeutic process. *Journal of Trauma and Dissociation, 9*, 349–367.

Howell, E. F. (1996). Dissociation in masochism and psychopathic sadism. *Contemporary Psychoanalysis, 3*, 427–455.

Howell, E. F. (2005). *The dissociative mind*. The Analytic Press.

Howell, E. F. & Itzkowitz, S. (2016). *The dissociative mind in psychoanalysis: Understanding and working with trauma*. Routledge.

Irigaray, L. (1977). *This sex which is not one* (C. Porter, Trans.). Cornell University Press.

Janet, P. (1886). Les actes inconscients et la mémoire et le dédoublement de la personnalité pendant le somnambulisme provoqué. *Revue Philosophique, 22*, 577–592.

Jones, A. L. (2015). A psychoanalytic reader's commentary: On erasure and negation as a barrier to the future. *Psychoanalytic Dialogues, 25*(6), 719–724.

Kanavou, A., Path, K., & Doll, K. (2016). Breaking the cycles of repetition: The Cambodian genocide across generations in Anlong Veng. In P. Gobodo-Madikizela (Ed.), *Breaking intergenerational cycles of repetition* (pp. 174–192). Creative Commons.

Katz, G. (1998). Where the action is: The enacted dimension of analytic process. *Journal of the American Psychoanalytic Association, 46*, 1129–1167.

Kestenberg, J. S. (1990). A metapsychological assessment based on an analysis of a survivor's child. In M. S. Bergmann & M. E. Jacovy (Eds.), *Generations of the Holocaust* (pp. 137–158). Columbia University Press.

Kestenberg, M. (1982). Psychoanalytic contributions to the problems of children of survivors from Nazi persecution. *Israel Annals of Psychiatry and Related Disciplines, 10*, 311–325.

Kestenberg, J. S. & Kestenberg, M. (1982). The background of the study. In M. Bergman & M. Jucovy (Eds.), *Generations of the Holocaust* (pp. 33–45). Basic Books.

Kierkegaard, S. (1937). *The concept of dread.* Princeton University Press.

Kogan, I. (1995). *The cry of mute children: A psychoanalytic perspective of the second generation of the Holocaust.* Free Association Books.

Kohler, B. (2012). Relational psychosis psychotherapy: A neuropsychoanalytic model. Paper presented at a meeting of the American Association of Psychoanalytic Physicians, Washington, DC.

Kohon, G. (1986). *The British school of psychoanalysis: The independent tradition.* Free Association Books.

Krondorfer, B. (2016). Unsettling empathy: Intercultural dialogues in the aftermath of historical and cultural trauma. In P. Gobodo-Madikizela (Ed.), *Breaking intergenerational cycles of repetition* (pp. 90–113). Creative Commons.

Krystal, H. (1985). Trauma and the stimulus barrier. *Psychoanalytic Inquiry, 5*(1), 131–161.

Kuriloff, E. A. (2013). *Contemporary psychoanalysis and the legacy of the Third Reich: History, memory, tradition.* Routledge.

La Capra, D. (2002). *Writing history, writing trauma.* Johns Hopkins University Press.

Lambourne, W. & Niyonzima, D. (2016). Breaking cycles of trauma and violence: Psychosocial approaches to healing and reconciliation in Burundi. In P. Gobodo-Madikizela (Ed.), *Breaking intergenerational cycles of repetition* (pp. 291–306). Creative Commons.

Langer, L. (1991). *Holocaust testimonies: The ruins of memory.* Yale University Press.

Laub, D. (1989). The empty circle: Children of survivors and the limits of reconstruction. *Journal of the America Psychoanalytic Association, 46*, 507–530.

Laub, D. (1992). Bearing witness or the vicissitudes of listening In S. Felman & D. Laub (Eds.), *Testimony: Crises of witnessing in literature, psychoanalysis and history* (pp. 57–74). Routledge.

Laub, D. (1995). Truth and testimony: The process and the struggle. In C. Caruth (Ed.), *Trauma: Explorations in memory* (pp. 61–75). John Hopkins University Press.

Laub, D. (2017). Listening to my mother's testimony. In J. Salberg & S. Grand (Eds.), *Wounds of history: Repair and resilience in the transgenerational transmission of trauma* (pp. 18–38). Routledge.

Laub, D. & Auerhahn, N. C. (1993). Knowing and not knowing massive psychic trauma: Forms of traumatic memory. *International Journal of Psychoanalysis*, *74*, 287–302.

Laub, D. & Podell, D. (1995). Art and trauma. *International Journal of Psychoanalysis*, *76*, 991–1005.

Layton, L. (2006). Racial identities, racial enactments, and normative unconscious processes. *Psychoanalytic Quarterly*, *75*, 237–269.

Layton, L. (2017). Racialized enactments and normative unconscious processes: Where haunted identities meet. In S. Grand & J. Salberg (Eds.), *Transgenerational trauma and the other: Dialogues across history and difference* (pp. 144–165). Routledge.

Layton, L. (2020). *Toward a social psychoanalysis: Culture, character, and normative unconscious processes*. Routledge.

Layton, L. & Goodman, D. (2014). Psychology and the other: The historical-political in psychoanalysis' ethical turn. *Psychoanalysis, Culture and Society*, *19*(3), 225–232.

Lazali, K. (2021). *Colonial trauma*. Polity Press.

Leary, J. D. (2005). *Posttraumatic slave syndrome: America's legacy of enduring injury and healing*. Upton Press.

Leary, K. (2002). Race in psychoanalytic space. In M. Dimen & V. Goldner (Eds.), *Gender in psychoanalytic space: Between clinic and culture* (pp. 313–329). Other Press.

Leary, K. (2012). Racial enactments in dynamic treatment. In S. Akhtar (Ed.), *The African American experience: Psychoanalytic perspectives* (pp. 403–415). Jason Aronson.

Lieberman, A. F. (2014). Giving words to the unsayable: The healing power of describing what happened. *Psychoanalytic Dialogues*, *24*, 277–281.

Liner, D. (2017). When the shadow of the Holocaust falls upon the analytic dyad. In S. Grand & J. Salberg (Eds.), *Transgenerational trauma and the other: Dialogues across history and difference* (pp. 59–80). Routledge.

Liotti, G. (2004). Trauma, dissociation and disorganized attachment: Three strands of a single braid. *Psychotherapy*, *41*(4), 472–486.

Lloyd, D. (1997). The memory of hunger. In D. Eng & D. Kazanjian (Eds.), *Loss: The politics of mourning* (pp. 205–227). University of California Press.

Lyons-Ruth, K. (2002). The two-person construction of defenses: disorganized attachment strategies, unintegrated mental states, and hostile/helpless relational processes. *Journal of Infant, Child and Adolescent Psychotherapy*, *2*, 107–119.

Lyons-Ruth, K. (2003). Dissociation and the parent-infant dialogue: A longitudinal perspective from attachment research. *Journal of the American Psychoanalytic Association*, *51*, 883–911.

Main, M. (1995). Recent studies in attachment: Overview, with selected implications for clinical work. In S. Goldberg, R. Muir, & J. Kerr (Eds.), *Attachment theory: Social, developmental and clinical perspectives* (pp. 407–474). The Analytic Press.

Main, M. & Hesse, E. (1990). Parents' unresolved traumatic experiences are related to infant disorganized attachment status: Is frightened and/or frightening parental behavior the linking mechanism? In M. T. Greenberg, D. Cicchetti, & E. M. Cummings (Eds.), *Attachment in the preschool years* (pp. 161–182). Chicago University Press.

Meares, R. (1998). The self in conversation: On narratives, chronicles, and scripts. *Psychoanalytic Dialogues, 8,* 875–891.

Menakem, R. (2017). *My grandmother's hands: Racialized trauma and the pathway to mending our hearts and bodies.* Central Recovery Press.

Mészáros, J. (2018) Ferenczi's paradigm shift in trauma theory. In A. Dimitrijevic, G. Cassullo & J. Frankel (Eds.), *Ferenczi's influence on contemporary psychoanalytic traditions* (pp. 115–121). Routledge.

Minuchin, L. (2018). Melanie Klein's development of, and divergence from, Sándor Ferenczi's ideas. In A. Dimitrijevic, G. Cassullo, & J. Frankel (Eds.), *Ferenczi's influence on contemporary psychoanalytic traditions* (pp. 190–194). Routledge.

Mitchell, J. (1973). *Psychoanalysis and feminism.* Vintage Books.

Mitchell, S. A. (1999). Attachment theory and the psychoanalytic tradition. *Psychoanalytic Dialogues, 9*(1), 85–107.

Moss, D. (2010). War stories. In A. Harris & S. Botticelli (Eds.), *First do no harm: Paradoxical encounters of psychoanalysis, warmaking and resistance* (pp. 243–250). Routledge.

Mucci, C. (2013). *Beyond individual and collective trauma: Intergenerational transmission, psychoanalytic treatment and the dynamics of forgiveness.* Karnac Press.

Mucci, C. (2018). Psychoanalysis for a new humanism: Embodied testimony, connectedness, memory and forgiveness for a "persistence of the human." *International Forum of Psychoanalysis, 27*(3), 176–187.

Mucci, C. (2022). *Resilience and survival: Understanding and healing intergenerational trauma.* Confer Books.

Neri, C. (2016). Field theory and transgenerational phantasies. In F. Borgogno, A. Luchetti, & L. M. Coe (Eds.), *Reading Italian psychoanalysis* (pp. 406–416). Routledge.

Newirth, J. (2016). A Kleinian perspective on dissociation and trauma: Miscarriages in symbolization. In E. F. Howell & S. Itzkowitz (Eds.), *The dissociative mind in psychoanalysis: Understanding and working with trauma* (pp. 107–117). Routledge.

Ogden, T. (1994). The analytic third: Working with intersubjective clinical facts. *International Journal of Psychoanalysis, 75,* 3–20.

Orange, D. M. (2011). *The suffering stranger: Hermeneutics for everyday clinical practice.* Routledge.

Ornstein, A. (2003). Survival and recovery: Psychoanalytic reflections. *Progress in Self Psychology*, *19*, 85–105.

Ornstein, A. (2004). *My mother's eyes*. Emmis Press.

Perroud, N., Rutembesa, E., Paoloni-Giacobino, A., Mutabaruka, J., Mutesa, L., Stenz, L., Malafossse, A., & Karege, F. (2014). The Tutsi genocide and transgenerational transmission of maternal stress: Epigenetics and biology of the HPA axis. *World Journal of Biological Psychiatry*, *15*(4), 334–345.

Pivnick, B. A., & Hassinger, J. A. (2023). The relational citizen as implicated subject: Emergent unconscious processes in the psychoanalytic community collaboratory. In R. Kabasakalian-McKay & D. Mark (Eds.), *Inhabiting implication in racial oppression and in relational psychoanalysis* (pp. 158–183). Routledge.

Poland, W. S. (2000). The analyst's witnessing and otherness. *Journal of the American Psychoanalytic Association*, *48*, 17–34.

Prager, J. (2016). Disrupting intergenerational transmission of trauma: Recovering humanity, repairing generations. In P. Gobodo-Madikizela (Ed.), *Breaking intergenerational cycles of repetition* (pp. 12–25). Creative Commons.

Prince, R. (2009). Psychoanalysis traumatized: The legacy of the Holocaust. *American Journal of Psychoanalysis*, *69*, 179–194.

Rachman, A. W. (1997). The suppression and censorship of Ferenczi's Confusion of tongues paper. *Psychoanalytic Inquiry*, *17*(4), 459–485.

Rand, N. T. (1994). Introduction. In N. Abraham & M. Török, *The shell and the kernel: Renewals of psychoanalysis* (pp. 1–22). University of Chicago Press.

Reis, B. (2005). The subject of history/The object of transference. *Studies in Gender and Sexuality*, *6*, 217–240.

Reis, B. (2009). Performative and enactive features of psychoanalytic witnessing: The transference as the scene of address. *International Journal of Psychoanalysis*, *90*(6), 1359–1372.

Reis, B. (2015). How deep the sky: Discussion of special issue on the evolution of witnessing: emergent relational trends in Holocaust studies. *Contemporary Psychoanalysis*, *51*(2), 333–347.

Ricaud, M. M. (2018). The Ferenczi-Balint filiation. In A. Dimitrijevic, G. Cassullo & J. Frankel (Eds.), *Ferenczi's influence on contemporary psychoanalytic traditions* (pp. 173–179). Routledge.

Richards, B. (2018). Exploring malignancies: Narcissism and paranoia today. *Psychoanalysis, Culture and Society*, *23*(1), 5–15.

Richman, S. (2006). Finding one's voice: Transforming trauma into autobiographical narrative. *Contemporary Psychoanalysis*, *42*, 639–650.

Richman, S. (2017). The pathologizing tilt: Undertones of the death instinct in relational trauma theory. In L. Aron, S. Grand, & J. Slochower (Eds.), *Decentering relational theory: A comparative critique* (pp. 92–116). Routledge.

Richman, S. (2020). Witness to war: Enlisting the creative process in working through trauma. *Psychoanalytic Perspectives*, *20*, 1–20.

Rosenkotter, L. (1982). The formation of ideals in the succession of generations. In M. S. Bergman & M. E. Jucovy (Eds.), *Generations of the Holocaust* (pp. 183–185). Basic Books.

Rothberg, M. (2008). Decolonizing trauma studies: A response. *Studies in the Novel*, *40*, 224–234.

Rothberg, M. (2019). *The implicated subject: Beyond victims and perpetrators.* Stanford University Press.

Rudnytsky, P. L. (2022). *Mutual Analysis: Ferenczi, Severn, and the Origins of Trauma Theory.* London & New York: Routledge.

Salberg, J. (2007). Hidden in plain sight: Freud's Jewish identity revisited. *Psychoanalytic Dialogues*, *17*(2), 197–217.

Salberg, J. (2015). The texture of traumatic attachment: Presence and ghostly absence in transgenerational transmission. *Psychoanalytic Quarterly*, *84*(1), 21–43.

Salberg, J. (2017). The texture of traumatic attachment: presence and ghostly absence in transgenerational transmission. In J. Salberg & S. Grand (Eds.), *Wounds of history: Repair and resilience in the transgenerational transmission of trauma* (pp. 77–101). Routledge.

Salberg, J. & Grand, S. (Eds.). (2017). *Wounds of history: Repair and resilience in the transgenerational transmission of trauma.* Routledge.

Sartre, J. P. (1981). *Existential psychoanalysis.* Regnery Press.

Scarry, E. (1985). *The body in pain: The making and the unmaking of the world.* Oxford University Press.

Schechter, D. (2003). Intergenerational communication of maternal violent trauma: Understanding the interplay of reflective functioning and posttraumatic psychopathology. In S. Coates, J. Rosenthal, & D. Schechter (Eds.), *September 11: Trauma and human bonds* (pp. 115–142). The Analytic Press.

Schechter, D. (2017). On traumatically skewed intersubjectivity. *Psychoanalytic Inquiry*, *37*, 251–264.

Schore, A. N. (2001). The effects of early relational trauma on the right brain development, affect regulation, and infant mental health. *Infant Mental Health Journal*, *22*, 201–269.

Schore, A. N. (2003a). *Affect regulation and disorders of the self.* W. W. Norton.

Schore, A. N. (2003b). *Affect regulation and the repair of the self.* W. W. Norton.

Shapiro, S. (1993). Clara Thompson: Ferenczi's messenger with half a message. In L. Aron & A. Harris (Eds.), *The legacy of Sándor Ferenczi* (pp. 159–174). The Analytic Press.

Slade, A. (2014). Imagining fear: Attachment, threat, and psychic experience. *Psychoanalytic Dialogues*, *24*, 253–266.

Slochower, J. (2004). *Holding and psychoanalysis: A relational approach.* Routledge.

Spence, D. (1982). *Narrative truth and historical truth.* Norton.

Spezzano, C. (1993) A relational model of inquiry and truth: The place of psychoanalysis in human conversation. *Psychoanalytic Dialogues, 3*, 177–209.

Stannard, D. E. (1992). *American Holocaust: The conquest of the new world.* Oxford University Press.

Stern, D. B. (2010). *Partners in thought: Working with unformulated experience, dissociation, and enactment.* Routledge.

Stern, D. B. (2012). Witnessing across time: Accessing the present from the past and the past from the present. *Psychoanalytic Quarterly, 81*, 53–81.

Stern, D. B. (2022). On coming into possession of oneself: Witnessing and the formulation of experience. *Psychoanalytic Quarterly, 91*, 639–667.

Stern, D. N. (1985). *Interpersonal world of the infant: A view from psychoanalysis and developmental psychology.* Basic Books.

Stern, D. N., Jaffe, J., Beebe, B., & Bennett, S. L. (1975). Vocalizing in unison and in alternation: Two modes of communication within the mother-infant dyad. *Annals of the New York Academy of Science, 19*(263), 89–100.

Stephens, M. A. (2022). We have never been white: Afropessimism, Black rage, and what the pandemic helped me learn about race (and psychoanalysis). *Psychoanalytic Quarterly, 91*(2), 319–347.

Stoute, B. (2019). Racial socialization and thwarted mentalization: Psychoanalytic reflections from the lived experience of James Baldwin's America. *American Imago, 76*(3), 335–357.

Stoute, B. (2021). Black rage: The psychic adaptation to the trauma of oppression. *Journal of the American Psychoanalytic Association, 69*(2), 259–290.

Sullivan, H. S. (1953). *The interpersonal theory of psychiatry.* Norton.

Taylor, F. (2023). *Unruly therapeutic: Black feminist writings and practices in the living room.* Norton Professional Books.

Thomas, N. K. (2009). Which horse do you ride? Trauma from a relational perspective, discussion of Prince's "The self in pain: The paradox of memory, the paradox of testimony." *American Journal of Psychoanalysis, 69*(4), 298–303.

Tracey, N. (2012). The autistic core in Aboriginal trauma: Breaking down or breaking out of the autistic defense. *Psychoanalysis, Culture and Society, 17*(4), 356–373.

Tronick, E. Z. (1989). Emotions and emotional communication in infants. *American Psychologist, 44*, 112–119.

Tronick, E. Z. (2017). *The neurobehavioral and social-emotional development of infants and children.* Norton.

Ullman, C. (2006). Bearing witness: Across the barriers in society and in the clinic. *Psychoanalytic Dialogues, 16*, 181–198.

Varea, R. G. (2011). A fire in the memory: Theatre, truth and justice in Argentina and Peru. In C. E. Cohen, R. G. Varea, & P. O. Walker (Eds.), *Acting together: Performance and the creative transformation of conflict* (Vol. 1, pp. 153–177). New Village Press.

Vaughans, K. (2015). To unchain haunting blood memories: Intergenerational trauma among African Americans. In M. O'Loughlin & M. Charles (Eds.), *Fragments of trauma and the social production of suffering: Trauma, history and memory* (pp. 277–290). Rowman & Littlefield.

Villanueva, M. (1989). Literature review. In E. Duran (Ed.), *Suicide handbook: Prevention and intervention with Native Americans* (pp. 13–36). Indian Health Service.

Volkan, V. (2017). Large-group identity and massive trauma. In J. Alpert & E. Goren (Eds.), *Psychoanalysis, trauma and community: History and contemporary reappraisals* (pp. 145–162). Routledge.

Walker, P. (2016). Acting together to disrupt cycles of violence: Performance and social healing. In P. Gobodo-Madikizela (Ed.), *Breaking intergenerational cycles of repetition* (pp. 325–343). Creative Commons.

Wikinski, M. (2018). Foreword. In K. Lazali (Ed.), *Colonial trauma* (pp. viii–x). Polity Press.

Williams, C. R. (2020, 26 June). You want a confederate monument? My body is a confederate monument. *New York Times*.

Winnicott, D. W. (1967). The location of cultural experience. *International Journal of Psychoanalysis, 48*, 368–372.

Woods, A. (2020). The work before us: Whiteness and the psychoanalytic institute. *Psychoanalysis, Culture & Society, 25*(2), 230–249.

Yehuda, R., Daskalakis, N. P., Bierer, L. M., Bader, H. N., Klengel, T., Holsboer, F., & Binder, E. B. (2015). Holocaust exposure induced intergenerational effects on FKBP5 methylation. *Biological Psychiatry, 80*(5), 372–380.

Index

Note: Page numbers followed by "n" denote endnotes

For Product Safety Concerns and Information please contact our EU
representative GPSR@taylorandfrancis.com
Taylor & Francis Verlag GmbH, Kaufingerstraße 24, 80331 München, Germany

www.ingramcontent.com/pod-product-compliance
Lightning Source LLC
Chambersburg PA
CBHW070348270326
41926CB00017B/4035